Mix It Up, Make It Nice

Mix It Up, Make It Nice

Secrets of a Tennis Mom

Betty Blake

Fay Publishing, LLC
Fairfield Connecticut

Published by Fay Publishing, LLC.

To order Mix It Up, Make It Nice: Secrets of a Tennis Mom, visit www.bookch.com.

Publisher's Cataloging-in-Publication Data

Blake, Betty.

    Mix it up, make it nice : secrets of a tennis mom / by Betty Blake.—1st ed.

    p. cm.

    ISBN 978-0-615-37375-1

    1. Biography. 2. Sports. I. Title.

Printed in the United States of America

First Edition

Credits:

  Jacket:
    Design by Susan Katz, sk@dotmediainc.com, www.dotmediainc.com

    Front Cover:
    James Blake*: © and photo by Stephen Danelian
    Betty Blake: © and photo by Susan Katz

    Spine:
    James Blake background*: © and photo by Stephen Danelian

    Back Cover:
    James Blake (white headband)*: © and photo by Ray Giubilo
    Four small photos: Courtesy Blake family collection

    Front Flap:
    James Blake background: © and photo by Ray Giubilo

    Back Flap:
    James Blake background*: © and photo by Stephen Danelian
    Betty Blake (with racket), Betty Blake*: © and photos by Susan Katz

    *James and Betty Blake are wearing Fila's Thomas Reynolds Collection, named after his father and inspired by James's contemporary sports lifestyle and keen sense of style. To see the entire collection, visit www.fila.com/us/eng/collections/thomas-reynolds

  Interior:
    Design by Ray Fusci, rayfusci@momentumtime.com

    Except as otherwise credited, all photos courtesy Blake family collection.

To Tom

Half a pound of tuppenny rice,
Half a pound of treacle.
Mix it up and make it nice,
Pop! goes the weasel.

—TRADITIONAL

On a small scale, Tom and I "mixed it up" and our sons have "made it nice" for us. On a larger scale, the American people "mixed it up" in 2008 and now we hope Barack Obama can turn this country around and "make it nice" for us all.

On an even larger scale, I hope someday the whole world will "mix it up" so all races and creeds could live in peace. That would truly "make it nice," for us and for future generations.

Acknowledgments

To Tom, and my sons Howard, Chris, Thomas and James. Without them, there would be no book.

I thank my friend Doug Smith for his encouragement and some helpful suggestions, and I thank my writing teachers at Fairfield University: Lyll Becerra de Jenkins, Ann Brophy, Ted Cheney and Andi Rierden.

And again, Tom—my alpha and omega.

Contents

Prologue

I NEVER DID AGREE that "nice guys finish last." I always thought it depended on what you meant by last.

On May 1 2006, James Blake feels on top of the world. With his mother and older brother Thomas by his side, he sits on the makeshift dais outside the Fairfield Warde High School tennis courts in Fairfield Connecticut, where he has logged more hours than on any other court in the world, and listens as one speaker after another tell anecdotes to illustrate why James has become known as a "nice guy."

His high school coach, John Honey, relates the moving moment when James, on a visit to his old school, singled out a fellow scoliosis sufferer and presented her with his outfit from the US Open, reducing her to tears. Ann Worcester, Director of the Pilot Pen Tournament in New Haven, mentions the clinics James gives for the underprivileged in New Haven and the endless autographs he signs. I could talk about the annual exhibition he and his brother give to benefit the Harlem Junior Tennis Program and the visits James makes to the children in the Shriners Hospital in Tampa. I think about how the acclaim he now enjoys has had little adverse effect on him. He still gets a big thrill from an occasion like this, seeing all his old friends, his former teachers as well as hordes of new friends and admirers—he's still a "nice guy."

James acknowledges the accolades, and then says wonderingly, "I can't believe how big a deal this is and how many people still care about me."

At the time, James held the rank of seventh-best tennis player in the world. He rose to that position in just a year and a half (from a ranking of below 200 at the end of 2004), with two titles in 2005 (Pilot Pen and Stockholm), two more in 2006 (Sydney and Las Vegas) as well as reaching the finals at the Masters at Indian Wells, where he lost to Roger Federer. So okay, this nice guy isn't first, but he's a long way from last.

The occasion is the dedication of these courts where from 1995-1998 James played for his high school tennis team, the Fairfield High Mustangs. The courts now bear a plaque proclaiming "The James Blake Courts—Home of the Mustangs." I sit next to James, barely hearing the praises heaped on my youngest son. I gaze at the courts remembering the good times my husband Tom and I enjoyed here with our sons Thomas and James, long before they ever thought of playing for their high school and certainly before they considered tennis as a career.

I recall our doubles games when James (the weakest player) played with his dad (the strongest) against Thomas and me. Our strategy was to keep the ball away from Tom and take advantage of little James. I remember warm summer nights when we would play until we could barely see the ball. I see Tom hitting one overhead after another and the boys scurrying back and forth trying to retrieve them. I recall James's frustration when he couldn't beat his mother; trying to teach him he couldn't return every shot, sometimes he should just applaud his opponent's good shot and go on to the next point; I remember our frustration when he didn't want to hear it.

I see them playing for the Mustangs. Thomas earned the number-one spot as a freshman, but James had to wait until his sophomore year for that honor, after his brother graduated. What a thrill it was to watch them playing on adjacent courts, Thomas, a senior, and James, a freshman, at one and two singles.

After the boys went to college, Tom and I spent many hours on these courts. We needed little more than a tennis court and a fine day to make us happy. I was no match for Tom, but we devised drills and games that worked for us. Much later, I see Tom struggling to hit with me after his cancer operation, trying desperately to get on the road to recovery—a recovery that never happened, for he died in July 2004, little more than a year after being diagnosed with stomach cancer. He missed seeing James's amazing recovery from a neck injury sustained that same year, and from the even more debilitating shingles that followed his father's death. He wasn't there to see James's triumphs in 2005 and 2006, when he rose to number four in the world. Now the tears start and I have to wrench myself back to the present and enjoy James's day with him.

With these courts just a 15-minute walk from our house, we never needed to join one of the many country clubs Fairfield has to offer. The high school courts were all we needed.

We moved to Connecticut when James was six and Thomas nine, but the Blake story begins even earlier. It begins on a run-down tennis court in Fay Park in the southwest corner of Yonkers, where Tom and I first met— two people from different countries, different races, born in different decades, but who found they had a lot in common—much more than their love of tennis.

Mix It Up, Make It Nice

Mix It Up, Make It Nice

There's a divinity that shapes our ends,
Rough-hew them how we will.

—WILLIAM SHAKESPEARE

Chapter 1:
A Perfect Union

ONE OF MY MOM'S favorite sayings from her huge store of truisms, clichés and Bible quotes was "What is to be will be." Considering our vastly different backgrounds—we grew up in different countries; he was 10 years younger than I; he was African American while I am Caucasian—I think fate had a hand in my meeting my husband Tom. Ironically, although neither of us thought too much about tennis until well into our adult lives, it was our mutual love of this game that brought us together.

Even though our early years were so different, we discovered we had been brought up with many of the same values. Offspring of hard-working, middle-class parents, for various reasons we had to deal with privations in our early lives. We both derived a strong work ethic from our parents, which we eventually passed on to our own sons. Oddly enough, as we gradually delved into each other's backgrounds, we discovered several similarities in the lives of our parents.

Me at age 1.

My formative years differed greatly from Tom's, not only because I lived in a different country but also because it was a different time. Just after my fourth birthday, England declared war on Germany. Although my hometown Banbury, a small market town in the middle of the country 72 miles from London, was considered one of the safer places to live, I still remember the fear when we heard the undulating wail of the siren, and the relief we felt at the monotonous sound of the all clear. Sometimes the siren sounded while we were in school, and we had to troop out to our designated shelters, carrying our gas masks that went everywhere with us.

Seven of us lived in a four-bedroom house with no heat (except three fireplaces) and no hot water. George Edward (Ed) and Phyllis Winifred (still known as "Nin" because as a toddler Ed was unable to say "Win"), the two oldest, were only 15 months apart. Albert was born six years later and I'm the youngest, three years younger than Albert. The baby in the family, I came in for plenty of teasing from my siblings, most of it from Albert, but even though he belittled me more than the others did, I would try to do anything and everything to please him. I idolized him. In fact, I laughed at his teasing because it seemed to amuse

2

him, and I liked to see him happy. He wanted nothing to do with me. When I first went to Banbury Grammar School, which he had attended for three years, he cautioned me if we met in the halls I must ignore him and tell no one I was his sister. Now, when I remind him of how he treated me, he feels tons of remorse, gives me a hug and tells me how much he loves me.

Mom and Dad were both in their late twenties when they wed. Music brought Thomas Misseldine and Gladys Healey together. Dad had an impressive baritone voice and often gave concerts. Mom (so the story goes) had longed for a piano in her youth, but had to wait until her 17th birthday, when her father bought one for her. She practiced so diligently that after two years she was able to give lessons. The romance began when she was asked to accompany Dad at several of his concerts. In one of life's cruel little ironies, their firstborn turned out to be completely tone deaf. Although the rest of us could carry a tune and we all took piano lessons, not one of us showed any particular musical talent. I

Gladys Healey, my mom.

stayed at it longest, taking lessons on and off for six years. I practiced on the same piano Mom had learned on—a black Strohmenger with several chipped ivories at the treble end where Ed cut his teeth.

Besides her music, Mom had a passion for sewing. She left school at age 14 to work in a sewing factory. She sewed so rapidly the management asked her to slow down—she was making too much in bonus wages. After she married and started raising a family, she took in sewing from the neighbors so she could always be home when we needed her. Even though she charged ridiculously low prices, the extra money helped supplement Dad's earnings as a police detective at the railway. She would make almost all our clothes. What she couldn't sew, she would knit. "I only wish I could make their shoes," I've heard her say.

Looking back on those days I can only marvel at the way my mom held the family together. With four children to take care of, an ailing husband and her mother who chose to live with us instead of her childless son and his wife or her youngest daughter who had only one child, life for her could not have been easy. She had to try to stretch the meager war rations to accommodate two hungry men. Dad, because of stomach ulcers, needed a special diet with plenty of eggs. The ration was one egg per person per week, so we supplemented it by keeping our own hens. Mom also had to try to keep peace between Gran and four active, noisy children—no easy task. Gran was a fastidious lady who constantly reminded us how much better behaved was her other grandchild, George. In fact, once when he came to visit and seemed to be enjoying himself, she told him, "If you stay here much longer, you'll be as bad as they are."

In January 1945, just before the war ended, Mom's life became more difficult when Dad unexpectedly died after what should have been a routine operation to remove stomach ulcers. I remember Albert and me coming down to breakfast that morning, racing down the stairs to get the best place by the fire. We sensed right away something was wrong. At first Mom couldn't bring herself to tell us, but finally she had no choice. Incredibly, she sent us to school as if nothing had happened. Just 9 years old, I can still see the tears dropping down onto my exercise book as I struggled with my lessons.

A few months earlier, Dad had signed a consent form for me to take the scholarship exam for entry to the grammar school at age 9 instead of 11, the usual age. Passing this exam was the only way to get into Banbury Grammar School. Mom advised against it thinking it would put too much pressure on me, but Dad reasoned if I failed, I would have a better chance next time. The results of the exam arrived in February, a few weeks after Dad died. He never knew I was one of only three students from our school to pass that year. Throughout my life, I have selfishly had a difficult time forgiving him for dying before he really knew me.

Knowing him for such a short space of time, I have often tried to sort out what I actually remember of Dad and what I have heard from family lore. I remember him giving me airplane rides on the front lawn, holding one arm and one leg and swinging me 'round and 'round 'til I was dizzy. I remember visits to his tiny office at the railway station, a wooden hut with a horseshoe nailed over the door where he would sometimes let us use his typewriter—a rare and wondrous treat. I remember stealing bits of bacon from his breakfast plate (only Dad

Thomas John Misseldine, my dad.

and Ed got bacon) and him pretending to scold me. I remember him singing *Bless This House* at Christmas while Mom played the piano. I remember he always kissed Mom goodbye when he left—I can't remember them ever arguing.

I also remember one terrible night—July 19th, their wedding anniversary—when Dad and I were biking home from the allotment (a plot of land where we grew vegetables). Only 7 but tall for my age, I must have grown out of my bike, for I was riding Mom's. Feeling pleased with myself, I rode too fast ahead of Dad, and fell onto the newly graveled road. When Dad picked me up, I caught sight of the gaping hole below my knee, just one trickle of blood oozing down.

Mix It Up, Make It Nice

Dad carried me the short distance to our house. Frightened by the wound I had seen, I hollered at the top of my voice. Doors opened as neighbors wondered what all the noise was about. As he laid me on the sofa I heard Dad growl, "I'll bust that bloody bike." All the siblings crowded around, Albert offered a cricket stump to keep the leg straight and someone must have sent for an ambulance (we had no phone). I stayed in the hospital for a week, bandages from my thigh to my toes, and I spent that entire summer in a wheelchair. Albert told me he went out the next day to look for my piece of flesh, but he didn't find it.

After that, Dad was only with us for one more summer. After he died, Mom lavished heaps of praise on me for my exploits, both academic and athletic, but it wasn't the same as applause from him. He had been so proud of anything Nin did. I felt cheated.

I had my first introduction to tennis when I attended the Grammar School where tennis was part of the physical education curriculum. So unlike Tom, who learned to play as an adult, I had the opportunity to learn the basics in my youth. At the time it didn't impress me, possibly because of the method of instruction. The physical education teacher lined us up in rows and made us practice endless phantom forehands and backhands. By the third lesson, she actually allowed us to try to hit a ball.

Memories of tennis in my youth remain vague. I recall summer evenings at the courts in the park. I remember Mom buying me a Slazenger racket, but what most sticks in my mind about those times is flirting with the boys after we played. I must have played enough to become somewhat proficient because I made the school team— barely—third doubles with my best friend Mary Watts. We made an odd-looking pair for by the time I was 13 I had finished growing and stood at 5'8". Mary was a diminutive 4'2" and extremely sensitive about it. I still have a snapshot of her taken between Maureen Kelly (also tall) and me where Mary insisted on standing on a box. Unfortunately, the box appears in the picture. Despite the discrepancy in our heights, we managed to win most of our matches.

Mary was the classic "poor little rich girl." Although our family had little to offer in the way of material possessions, especially after Dad died, Mary loved coming to our house. Her parents owned a public house, *The Prince of Wales*, so they were never home in the evenings. Tragically, her older brother and sister had died within six months of each other in their teens, Thelma of gangrene after a biking accident and John of a rare liver disease. Mr. and Mrs. Watts heaped tons of material goods on their remaining child but that didn't compensate for the

Me and Mary Watts (my tennis partner). "The long and the short of it."

lack of family life. While I was jealous of her for the lavish presents she received at Christmas and birthdays—the five-pound boxes of Tobler chocolates, the brand-new Raleigh bike as well as her beautifully furnished home and expensive clothes—I believe she would have given it all up for a life like mine. Albert liked to tease her, too. When he saw her coming around the corner, he would run to the door and put his foot behind it so it came back and hit her when she tried to push it open. She didn't mind—it made her feel like part of the family.

Although I enjoyed playing tennis, my real passion throughout my years at the grammar school was track and field. I vividly recall my introduction to it. The whole class took part in an initial practice to find out who could reach the standards the school set for running and jumping. They set the high-jump bar at 3'6". One girl after another tried and failed. The bar kept clanking down and they kept replacing it. The youngest in the class at age 9, and painfully shy, I waited for my turn on the opposite side. All the other girls jumped with their right leg first. I preferred the left. Someone finally noticed me standing alone, and I got my turn. After I sailed easily over the bar, I elicited a lot more interest and got many more turns as they gradually raised the bar for those few who cleared it. So began my six-year passion for track.

Besides jumping, I found I could also outrun most of my contemporaries. The youngest pupil in the school, I won the 75 yards under 12 race at age 9, then won it twice more for an unprecedented three years, setting and then breaking the record. At the annual Sports Day in July, the school presented three trophies—junior, middle and senior. If those trophies still exist, you could find my name etched at least once on all of them. The engravers must have winced at having to fit in another "Betty Misseldine."

Me and Maureen Kelly.
Sports day, 1951.

My love for track and field events reached such proportions I began reading every magazine I could find on the subject. I memorized records in every event; I even mystified my mom by wheedling her into to buying me a pair of running spikes. She had no idea such items existed.

In my last two years at the school, the long jump became my specialty. My friend Maureen Kelly, who excelled at the high jump, and I traveled all over the county with the school track team (mostly boys, which made it more attractive), competing in various events. We spent a week in Southampton representing our county at the Junior Olympics. Families volunteered to house us, treating us like celebrities. They held an opening ceremony with the athletes parading around the track just like the real Olympics. In our brand-new tracksuits (our first), we felt like we had arrived.

With all this glory, I had little time for tennis. In the autumn and winter I played field hockey, where I could use my speed at the wing position. I have fond memories of tearing up and down the field on frosty mornings, the ground like iron under my cleats, trying to impress the boys on the sidelines who cheered us on. It's more likely they were admiring our short gym tunics rather than our athletic prowess, but we didn't care as long as they came to watch.

This all ended when Mom decided we should immigrate to America. After my father's untimely death at age 47 my mom devoted her life to her children. Nin had moved to Jefferson City Missouri to stay with friends with whom she had become acquainted through letters, and Albert had joined her a few years later. They didn't want to come back, so Mom decided we belonged there, too. Ed remained in England, but I was too young to have any say in the matter.

If I had had a choice I probably would have stayed home. Knowing it was only a visit I went willingly two years earlier when Albert came with us. I had relished these last two years at

"The day I left Banbury."
Me, Maureen Kelly,
Mary Watts, Christine
Stevens, Audrey Busby,
Anne Woodruff. Nicknamed
"the Gaggle" by our
headmaster.

school, doing well both academically and athletically, so I felt loath to leave my friends. Despite the long break from school while we visited the US, I passed the maximum number of subjects in my O Levels, and then went into the sixth form where two years of study culminates in the A-level exam to determine entry into a university. When Mom decided to immigrate I needed only one more year before the exam. I enjoyed learning and, unlike my siblings, wanted to experience university life. The move was doubly painful because I knew Dad would have supported me in this.

So we sailed again for the New World, this time on the Queen Elizabeth. From New York we made the seemingly endless train journey to Jefferson City. "How can you go so far without coming to the sea?" my mom wondered.

A few months after we arrived I met George Walker, a young sailor from New York. Friends of my sister had arranged a blind date for us, thinking we would have a lot in common because his parents came from England. An extremely personable young man, he did prove easy to talk to and at the end of the evening I felt I had finally found a friend. Unfortunately after a few days he left for an 18-month tour of duty in Hawaii. Throughout that time we wrote to each other and became so well acquainted that when he came back to the States he stopped off in Missouri on his way to New York and insisted I go with him. A few months later we married.

I soon discovered correspondence is not a good foundation for a marriage. I often compared George to an iceberg—for the one-fifth I knew about him, four-fifths remained submerged. After the first year the marriage deteriorated rapidly but that's another story, the best part of which is the two sons it produced. Howard was born on Mother's Day 1955 and Chris arrived in September nine years later. Both now realize what I went through with their father and often express their appreciation for my being there while he was virtually an absentee father.

Although I was initially concerned about Howard's development (he was 3 years old before he could talk in sentences), he is now Dr. Walker, with a doctorate in education from Rutgers University. Married with a wife and two daughters he lives in New Jersey where he is the principal of an elementary school. Chris graduated from Tulane (which he attended on a full tennis scholarship) and now works for an insurance company. He lives with his partner and their two dogs in Dallas Texas.

Howard holding Chris.

I spent two unhappy years in Missouri, which may have contributed to my willingness to go with George. I found New England much more to my liking. The countryside around Hastings-on-Hudson where George's parents lived reminded me of the English countryside. I became acquainted with a lot of different places for we moved many times during our 18 years together—from New York to New Jersey, to Yonkers, then Riverdale, a few years in Wethersfield Connecticut, then back again to Yonkers.

With my marriage in decline, I looked for other diversions. I decided to revive my interest in tennis. Our first apartment in Yonkers was close to Trevor Park where I would often walk Howard in his stroller and watch the activity on the four tennis courts. Though he was not overly enthusiastic, I convinced George we should buy permits and start to play. Rusty at first, I persevered and later became the local singles champion, a title I held for several years. George soon lost interest but tennis became my therapy. Hitting the ball as hard as possible helped me through years of desperation.

Our last move, back to Yonkers after two years in Connecticut, was to an apartment in the extreme southwest corner of town. At this point the marriage was virtually over and George and I were going our own ways. I still enjoyed playing tennis and soon found two courts in Fay Park, immediately behind the apartment house. The park sits behind graffiti-covered P.S. 27, between a home for wayward children on one side and the apartment buildings on the other. It boasts a huge football field, a baseball diamond, two basketball courts and a large playground, all of which take care of the popular activities in the area.

Tennis with its reputation as upper-class recreation had few fans here. Thus, the two run-down tennis courts seemed a little out of place in this setting, and indeed they saw use for many activities other than tennis. Hockey enthusiasts removed the nets and turned them into a rink; dog owners let their pets romp leashless inside the high fences; roller skaters enjoyed the flat surface; young children used them for the various games they invented. All this activity took its toll, and we few stalwarts who used the courts for their intended purpose often had to deal with bad bounces off the pockmarked surface.

Every Saturday and Sunday morning whenever the weather permitted (and sometimes when it didn't), a group of us gathered at these courts. We never arranged games or times—whoever showed up first played first, and pairing for doubles was random. If it rained the night before we brought brooms, but we often had more to deal with than water on the courts. On several occasions we had to search for the nets vandals had removed and disposed of in various areas of the park, and one morning after a holiday weekend the first arrivals found both courts smeared with large quantities of mustard and relish.

It was at Fay Park that I first met Tom. He was not a part of this group until through an ironic twist of fate I invited him to join us. One day while taking care of my friend's dress boutique, Tom's wife came into the shop. I knew her slightly and apparently she knew I played tennis. "Poor Tommy," she said. "He's dying to play tennis, but no one invites him into their games." I assured her we would welcome him into our group at Fay Park.

Tom accepted the invitation. A newcomer to tennis, he had quickly developed a passion for it, investing in lessons and equipment. He lived close to Fay Park but apparently had not known of the two courts there, for he had sat with his racket at several other public courts in Yonkers and never had the chance to play. He welcomed the opportunity to test his new skill.

Tom's path to tennis differed sharply from mine. He grew up in Yonkers New York where he attended Gorton High School and played on two varsity teams (basketball and football). I don't recall him ever mentioning the tennis team, but I believe it would never have occurred to him to try out for it. In those days tennis belonged to the white country-club crowd and opportunities for young African Americans to learn the game were rare. (When I offered to teach the game to a group of mostly Black teens at Leake & Watts, the children's home behind Fay Park, they initially laughed at me and dubbed it "a faggot game." I would guess that might have been how Tom and his high school friends viewed it.)

Tom was the second of four boys in a family where both parents worked full time. His father James, after first trying his hand at the fur trade, became a policeman (like my dad) and his mother began work in a sewing factory (like my mom), before working many years with the telephone company. We also discovered our mothers were both named Gladys. James and Gladys were childhood sweethearts. They met in their early teens, married in 1944 and enjoyed 59 years together before diabetes and congestive heart failure took their toll on Gladys.

Richard, their oldest son, and Tom, born two years later, both in February, grew up to be total opposites. Richard had a happy-go-lucky nature while Tom became more introspective as he grew older. Russell was born five years later, and Martin, the youngest, two years later.

I became only slightly acquainted with Richard and Martin, but I remember the pride Tom felt in his brother

Russell. We would often watch him play baseball and whenever he hit a home run, Tom became so excited you would think he hit it.

All four boys learned the meaning of responsibility early in life. They had to help with chores around the house, and as soon as they were able they found various ways to earn money. As soon as they were old enough, Richard and Tom shared an early-morning paper route. They would start at 4 a.m. so it didn't interfere with school. Either their father or Uncle Earl would go with them. In an effort to teach them the value of money, Tom's father insisted on his sons donating one dollar of every paycheck to their mother, a practice Tom also insisted on when his sons began earning.

Tom learned his lesson well. During our years together, he managed money wisely; sometimes, I thought, too wisely. He would have so much deducted from his paycheck I would sometimes complain we needed the money now.

"We have to save for our retirement," he would tell me.

Ironically (and sadly) I remember Mom telling me Dad used to say that, too. Both would have done well to listen to my mom when she recited another of her favorite Bible quotes—"Sufficient unto the day is the evil thereof." Tom's thrift proved a good influence on our boys. They both opened bank accounts as soon as they began to earn.

Another similarity in our families was the emphasis placed on education. My father and Tom's father both appreciated the life-long importance of learning and drummed it into their offspring. Because of this early training Tom and I, for various reasons each missing the opportunity for higher education at the normal age, pursued it during our years together. Tom received his bachelor's degree from the College of New Rochelle in 1981 and later went on to earn an MBA from Sacred Heart University. I finally received a bachelor's degree (begun 40 years earlier in Missouri) in 1992 from Fairfield University.

From high school, Tom signed up for the Air Force, following the example of his father and Richard. Russell and Martin joined the Army. Martin contemplated making it his career, but had a change of heart and left after 11 years. Tom spent some time in Turkey where he met Ray Pitts, who remained his best friend after they both left the service. On the base in Turkey, only 5 percent of the servicemen were Black, so naturally they banded together.

Ray, a graduate of Fisk University, grew up on the college campus where his father taught. In his youth he had access to tennis courts and his father taught him how to play. Ray introduced Tom to tennis in exchange for tips about the finer points of basketball. (Because tennis brought Tom and me together, Ray now claims credit for James's existence.) Whenever Tom found a new endeavor he felt worthwhile, he pursued it zealously. Those first few lessons whetted his appetite, and by the time I met him his main goal in life seemed to be to improve his tennis game.

Ray and Tom often played with one of the white instructors on the base, and would sometimes socialize after they played. Seeing Ray wearing a black armband after Martin Luther King's assassination, he apologized for the murder. At that, Tom asked him, "Why would you apologize? It involves you, too." That remark cemented what was becoming a close friendship between Ray and Tom.

Before going into the service Tom had begun training as a beautician, but he abandoned this in favor of a position as a repairman for gas sterilizers with 3M Company where he could make use of skills acquired in the Air Force. He stayed with the same company throughout his life, and worked his way up to Sales Manager for the surgical division. A conscientious and loyal worker, he won many awards during the 37 years he worked for the same company. Knowing of his earlier training, I often pressed him into service with the hairdryer.

Tom became a regular at Fay Park on weekends and sometimes played for the entire morning. He never seemed to tire. As we became better acquainted, I realized when he decided to learn something he would go all out to become the best he could be at it—a trait he later instilled in our two sons. He invested in a tennis lesson once a week and wanted to play more than just on weekends. He asked everyone in the group, but none left work early enough. With only a part-time job, I could spare the time. I found few people to play with me during the day, so I welcomed the chance to hit with Tom whenever he could get off work early. When I first met him, I could hold my own with most of the men in our group. In fact as the only female in the group, they dubbed me "Our Lady of Fay." Tom told me later when he first came to the park he heard I was the one to beat.

During the long days of summer we often played until darkness fell. Sometimes others of the group came to the courts and we played doubles, but I recall playing a lot of singles with Tom for many years. Over that time span he became much better while my game stayed the same. At first I won most of the time, then we went through a period where we played evenly, but soon he beat me all the time. Throughout our life together he maintained there is no substitute for hard work—another trait he drummed into our sons. The dramatic improvement in his tennis certainly supported that theory.

During those years ours was a comfortable relationship. Some evenings when it became too dark to see the ball, we would sit for a while on the wall surrounding the courts, talking and watching the sun go down, while the trees on the horizon turned purple in the twilight. He often seemed sad and his eyes conveyed that sadness. Expressive and deep set, they seemed to embody the accumulated grief of his race. We often touched on this subject, and some of his stories helped to open my eyes to the grievous injustices endured by African Americans. At the time I had a part-time job at Leake & Watts, the children's home behind Fay Park. Most of the children there were Black and he helped give me a much better understanding of their feelings. We found a large variety of other topics to discuss and I left with the warm feeling of having found a new friend.

Tom at Fay Park.

That was how it began. Two people from vastly different cultures and backgrounds became friends through a mutual love of tennis. Little by little we discovered we had a lot more in common, but for many

17

years tennis was the only link Tom and I had with each other. We both led our own lives away from the courts. After I separated from my husband I became friendly with several other men. I had endured years of being put down and belittled by my husband and I felt flattered by their attentions. Tom sometimes spoke of his marriage. He seemed determined to make the best of what I gathered was a bad situation. I rarely asked him about it—just listening when he felt like talking.

Eventually he and his wife separated, but for a long time after we both still led separate lives. I often played doubles with him in our friendly games at Fay. We made a good combination—I was steady in the backcourt, keeping the ball in play until he could use his net skills to put it away. Since we did well in these games, he suggested we play mixed doubles in some American Tennis Association (ATA) tournaments in our area. He had been playing some singles events and he wanted to try the doubles; or maybe he just wanted company on the long rides.

Me at Fay Park with Tom in the background.

The ATA, formed in 1916 by Black businessmen, college professors and physicians, is the African American answer to the United States Tennis Association, which at the time denied Black athletes access to their events. Sadly, most of the early events had to take place on Black college campuses because hotels (especially in the South) would not accommodate large groups of Black players. The ATA now has nine sections, all of which offer a variety of programs, tournaments and opportunities for junior development.

The first such tournament we entered took place in New Jersey. Tom had suggested I might as well enter the women's singles as well. When he saw the draw, he wished he hadn't talked me into it. My first opponent was the top seed, a young girl named Leslie Allen who at the time was the number-one Black junior in the country. This may have been her first adult tournament.

"Just go out and play your game," Tom advised me, not too convincingly.

I did just that, and Leslie, used to playing hard-hitting juniors who go for their shots and make their share of errors, was not ready for my steady, consistent method of just getting the ball back one more time. Hitting with Tom I had learned to handle pace. Becoming ever more frustrated, at one point Tom, watching behind the fence, heard her mutter, "You're not going to let this old lady beat you." I did beat her, but that was certainly the only time I would have had any chance, for Leslie went on to play on the tour, rose to number 16 in the world, and acquitted herself well at all of the Grand Slams.

We found we could hold our own with most of the mixed-doubles pairings and often reached the semis or the finals. While driving to these tournaments, our friendship deepened and became more meaningful for both of us. We never seemed to tire of talking to each other (this held true throughout all of our years together), and as we delved deeper into each other's feelings and experiences we grew closer. However, uncertain of the reception we would get, neither of us had the nerve to express these feelings. We have often reminisced about this, of how we looked forward to the drives home and how we didn't want them to end.

Mix It Up, Make It Nice

One of the reasons for our success in these tournaments was I felt comfortable playing with Tom. He never berated me for missing a shot as many partners do, especially, we noticed, when the partners were married. He just encouraged me to make the next shot and with that attitude I usually did. We would talk over our strategy during the warm-up after we had sized up our opponents. Usually the woman had the weaker game, so we would agree three out of four shots would go to her. As we got ready to play, I would ask the usual question, "Three out of four?" If the woman looked particularly weak, he would say with a grin, "How about four out of four?"

Realizing we had similar interests, we began to see each other off the tennis court. We both loved books and music and enjoyed browsing the bookstores in Greenwich Village. I introduced him to the music I enjoyed and through him I came to appreciate classical guitar and jazz. Tom had become a vegetarian so we talked a lot about food and he would take me to his favorite health food stores. Never a huge fan of meat, he convinced me I could get protein from other sources, so gradually I became a vegetarian. We found we had simple tastes, often making a meal of only a crusty loaf of black bread and a hunk of sharp cheese.

For a long time before we admitted it to each other, our feelings had progressed beyond friendship. Apparently this became obvious to others before we acknowledged it. One evening we visited Tom's best friend Ray Pitts in New Jersey. It turned slightly embarrassing when Ray and his wife Janice contrived to leave us alone in the apartment. We just looked at each other, wondering when they would come back. We listened to some music for a while, but eventually decided to leave.

Since we had enjoyed some success in the ATA mixed-doubles events, I asked Tom if he would be my partner in the Yonkers annual tournament. I had won the singles title several times but never won the mixed doubles, despite playing it with a variety of different partners. The pair who won it each year seemed to have a lock on it. Tom felt confident we could displace them. We won our way to the finals and sure enough we had to play the reigning champs Claire Schwartz and Marty Geller in the finals. In the last set when our victory seemed assured, all I could think about was when we won I would throw caution to the winds and give Tom a hug and a kiss. He must have had the same idea. We won, and that kiss of triumph meant much more to me than the trophy, although I do treasure that award more than most because of the memories it evokes.

That was in July 1975. One evening in August we drove to Greenwich Village for no particular reason than to walk the narrow streets, browse the bookstores and be together. We treated ourselves to a falafel with tahini sauce and ate as we strolled, taking in the sidewalk artists and listening to the street musicians. We stopped to look in a window displaying the kinds of merchandise you find in the Village. He seemed interested but I had something else on my mind. I don't know if it was the balmy night, the setting or the comfort and warmth of being with Tom, but I decided we had to clear the air.

"Tom," I began, a little hesitantly. He turned from the window and from the expression in his eyes I could tell he knew what I was about to say. He took my hand, pulled me away from the window and gently kissed me.

Now we realized this should have happened long ago. Both so delighted with ourselves for finally bringing it into the open, we started giggling like teenagers. For the rest of the walk our feet barely touched the ground. We held hands and kept looking at each other and grinning like imbeciles. Driving home up the West Side Highway, Tom was bubbling over. He told me he felt like singing but he didn't have a good voice, so would I mind? I felt like joining in, but my voice is worse than his. To this day, every time I drive up that highway past the Cloisters I remember that night—the beginning.

The next day Tom arrived at the courts with two roses, one in full bloom, the other a perfect bud. "This one is now," he said, pointing to the full-blown rose, "The other is the future." Normally I'm not overly sentimental, but I still have the paper those roses were wrapped in.

Mix It Up, Make It Nice

Eventually that bud blossomed in ways we could never have imagined. We had enjoyed being just friends for so long, and I can see now this is probably the best foundation for a marriage, for we stayed friends until the end. When our feelings deepened into love, that friendship remained. Tom, though not overly vocal about his feelings, would often hand me a greeting card on no particular occasion. I still have one that admirably expressed the depth of our feelings for each other—"Even when I don't like you sometimes, I still love you all of the time." Our love had such a firm foundation minor spats (rare in our life together) couldn't shake it.

One obstacle perceived more by others than by us was our disparate heritages. When I was with Tom, I would often forget the difference in our complexions. It took the reactions of others to bring it home to me. When I looked at him, I saw the inner man and would forget we didn't look alike. I hardly noticed when some people stared too long at us walking together, so obviously enjoying each other's company, but Tom, no stranger to racism, would become enraged. I've seen him turn to the offending person and bare his teeth, "I've got good teeth, too," he would say, alluding to the way slaves were selected. I liked to think they looked in envy because, obviously in love, we seemed so happy together, but I realize now how naïve that was.

Both a little hesitant to enter again into a serious relationship, we separated for a time to try to sort out our feelings. We soon realized we were much happier together than apart, and decided our feelings for each other were deep enough to overcome any obstacles others tried to put in our paths. Early in 1976, we became more than tennis partners.

Heaven lies about us in our infancy!

—WILLIAM WORDSWORTH

Chapter 2:
Yonkers Idyll

THE FIRST FEW YEARS Tom and I spent together proved a little chaotic. After living in an apartment in Yonkers for several years, we managed to save enough for a down payment on our first house. It just happened the house we chose was on St. Andrews Place in southwest Yonkers, just below the Riverdale/Yonkers line and about a five-minute walk from Fay Park where Tom and I first met.

We moved into the house in the summer of 1979. Our first son Thomas was two and a half, and we expected another child in January 1980. At the time this was a street in flux. Respectable homeowners, mostly older people, lived on the east end while low-rent apartments occupied the west end. Our house, made of white stone trimmed with imported Italian marble, ornate terraces in front and on the sides and an impressive oak-paneled

Our house in Yonkers.

front door, graced the middle of the block. It comprised two large rooms and an enormous kitchen, with two smaller rooms downstairs and three huge bedrooms upstairs. It also had a large basement that doubled as a playroom, and two bathrooms. A different-looking house, it stood out as the most elegant on the street, which probably accounted for the three break-ins we endured during the six years we lived there. From the outside, the unsuspecting burglars might have thought we had something worth stealing. I recall our sons' friends tended to look up to us as the wealthier residents of the neighborhood and loved to be invited in to play when rain kept them out of the park.

At the time we moved in, my 14-year-old son Chris and I were involved in a national tennis tournament sponsored by the Equitable Insurance Company. A family tournament, it paired parents with their children. Playing in the mother-son category, we won the local segment in August, and in September moved on to national competition held in conjunction with the US Open. We played four matches against teams from various parts of the country and managed to win them all. No one knew of my condition until we had won the trophy—but they didn't disqualify us for being mother and two sons. In pictures of the presentation, I'm the only one wearing warm-ups. Therefore, James really received his introduction to tennis while still *in utero*.

Yonkers Idyll

Playing in this tournament helped keep me from worrying about my doctor's dire predictions for our baby. When he told me of my condition, knowing my age (43) he advocated an early abortion. He told me how tiny and insignificant the baby was at this stage, and warned I risked having a baby with water on the brain or Down's syndrome. Positive, and so sure of himself, he seemed certain I would comply. I looked for another opinion. I talked with Father José Vilaplana, a Spanish priest at St. Peter's in Yonkers. I had never met Father José, but his sermons impressed me. I once went to a Spanish mass by mistake and, though I know almost no Spanish, I got more out of that sermon than many I've heard in English—he so obviously felt what he was saying. Father José told me I would never forgive myself if I did what the doctor advocated. I knew that. I just wanted someone in authority to tell me.

When pregnant with Thomas at age 41, I had endured amniocentesis (a test that examines fetal DNA for genetic abnormalities) at that same doctor's suggestion. I did what he prescribed without question, thinking, as we often do, doctors know best. Had I inquired further about the procedure, I could have spared myself the inconvenience. By the time they gave me the good news the baby was normal, I was just under the legal limit for abortion and Thomas was kicking vigorously. The result only served to put our minds at rest—under no condition would we have acted on it. Because of this, again against doctor's orders, I refused to go through amnio three years later. Instead, we relied on prayer and hope.

On December 27, the day before James's birth, Tom had booked two hours of court time at the indoor facility in Hastings. I went along to watch. Before the two hours ended, his partner tired and Tom beckoned me onto the court for the last 15 minutes. He may have had an ulterior motive, for remembering the healthy tax refund he received for Thomas, due in January but born on December 29, he had been encouraging me to give birth early again. If it were a ploy, it worked. I hadn't hit for a few months so it felt good to swing a racket again, until after about 10 minutes I had to excuse myself and go to the ladies' room. My water had broken—James was practically born on a tennis court.

The next day James Riley Blake came into the world. I had insisted on having no drugs or painkillers and my doctor (a woman, bless her) went along with my wishes, so I was fully awake. With Tom by my side, I put my first anxious question to him, "Is he all right?"

"He's beautiful," he assured me, "all the right numbers of fingers and toes." His eyes shone above the surgical mask, and we shared a moment of ecstasy. Unfortunately, the doctor who first counseled me had retired, so he never knew how wrong were his predictions about our youngest son.

James showed early signs of unusual athletic ability, but being my fourth son, all of whom possess good coordination, I paid scant attention to it. Before he could walk, he invented games involving hitting objects with a stick. He had little use for the corn popper section of his Fisher-Price toy, but he put the handle to good use. He unscrewed it from its base and used it to hit tennis balls the length of our kitchen, then he would crawl to the other end and hit them back. He rarely missed making contact. With Thomas in pre-school and James happily whacking tennis balls, I enjoyed several peaceful hours.

As the boys grew older, they found ways to amuse themselves at the tennis courts while Tom and I played. They would find sticks and hit rocks or bottle caps into the trees, seeing who could hit the farthest. My friend Herb Koizim, coming to the court one day saw James doing this and remarked, "You'll hit anything with a stick won't you, James?" Three-year-old James gravely considered the question and replied, "Anything but doo-doo." Herb still loves to tell that story.

At age 5-1/2, Thomas began first grade at St. Margaret's in Riverdale. James, aged 2-1/2, went with me when I volunteered for lunch duty. For the first half hour he ran around happily with Thomas and his friends in the smaller playground. Then we went to the upper school playground. Here, James amused the older boys by throwing a tennis ball as high as he could up the side of the building. A lofty structure, he aimed for the roof and almost made it. He attracted quite an audience, and they kept supplying him with another ball so he could try again. He did this until the boys went back into class, then he climbed back into his stroller and we went home for his afternoon nap.

I find it difficult to remember everything about those six years we spent in Yonkers. I do remember being extremely happy. We had our own beautiful house, two wonderful sons, and I had found my soulmate, who also proved to be an outstanding father. Yet when the media began to take an interest in James in 2001, reporters had a field day describing his "humble" beginnings. They would come up with a tiny grain of truth and embellish it until it sounded nothing like our family. They talked about the "mean streets" or "crime-infested streets" of Yonkers, conjuring up images of muggings, prostitution, drug busts and various other mayhem. It wasn't like that.

Thomas and James enjoyed normal, happy childhoods. I doubt if they ever felt deprived (except perhaps when we refused to buy the latest Nintendo cartridge) as these stories liked to imply. We did take some precautions. We accompanied them when they went "trick or treating" on Halloween, and we had to be wary during the weeks leading up to July 4. Some of the fireworks sounded more like bombs. However, these seemed minor problems.

An English publication in 2002 went a step further and wrote a piece entitled "Ghetto Master." It described James as "the ghetto kid who escaped the privations of his youth." The article further quotes James as saying he thought it was normal to have bars on doors and windows. James lived in Yonkers from his birth until he turned 6. Being so young, he must have forgotten we had no bars on our house, not even after the break-ins. After one of the break-ins, we did reinforce the front door with a steel plate, which greatly detracted from its looks. (The bars came later, after we left.) He may have been confusing us with the house next door, the home of an elderly couple who did feel the need for bars on their windows. In this article James also talked about coming home after a break-in. Not overly concerned, his main worry was his stickball bat, which happily the burglars had not touched. Our boys were too young to worry about danger, and I think it helped that Tom and I showed no real concern.

I'm reminded of how my brother Albert and I felt during the early years of World War II. Both too young to understand the gravity of the situation, we implicitly believed Mom when she reminded us England is known as the motherland and Germany *der Vaterland* (the fatherland), and when mother and father fight, mother always wins. With this assurance, we knew England couldn't lose. In the selfish way of children, to us the end of the war only meant we would finally get everything Mom had promised "when the war ends" and we could now have more than one chocolate bar per week. In the same way, for our children the move to Fairfield meant now they could go out without an adult and they could play stickball in the street. They hadn't lost sleep about being gunned down on their way to the park, as some of those articles seemed to imply.

"From Harlem to Harvard" became another favorite headline in more than one publication. We never lived in Harlem and we didn't appreciate the tacit implication that someone from Harlem attending Harvard verges on the miraculous, sort of like the surprise reporters (and others) show when an African American speaks articulately. Tom and I did play indoor tennis in Harlem, at the 369th Armory, which became a special place for us and remains so to this day. We both volunteered in the junior programs, so Thomas and James received their early tennis instruction there.

My second son Chris is amused and slightly indignant when he reads accounts such as I have described. "How can they say these kids are deprived?" he asks. "They're living in the lap of luxury compared to how Howard (his older brother) and I grew up. We were the deprived ones." He's right. I became a single parent when Chris was 7, with an ex-husband who contributed nothing towards our upkeep. I changed my part-time position to full time so I could pay the rent, and what I earned from giving private tennis lessons helped put food on the table, with little left over for luxuries. Fortunately I had taught both boys how to play tennis, and they became good enough to get tennis scholarships to college—Howard, a partial tennis to Fordham, which coupled with a Regents scholarship took care of all the bills, and Chris a full tennis to Tulane. I recall Howard saying as he filled out his college financial forms, "Just stay poor, Mom, and we'll be okay."

Getting back to Yonkers and outdoor tennis, we spent much of our time at Fay Park. I would load up the stroller with stickball bats, various kinds of balls, tennis rackets and anything else that might keep them amused. I took the rackets in case I found someone to hit with me and in case Thomas and James felt like trying their hand at tennis. This only happened if there was nothing more exciting to do. Whenever a group of boys organized a game of stickball they wanted to play. At first the older boys seemed skeptical of including little James in the games, but when they saw how he could swing a bat, he became one of the first to be picked when they chose up sides. They played in the playground next to the tennis courts. A ball over the high tennis court fence was a home run—if the ball landed on the other side of the net it was a grand slam. Thomas, much bigger and stronger than his brother, hit home runs regularly, but the first time James hit one over the fence caused quite a stir.

When they needed some quiet time, they played a curious game called Skullsy. They searched for discarded plastic bottle caps, which they then filled with candle wax. They all brought their favorite caps to the park. The game entailed sliding them around and hitting other caps on an elaborate chalk-drawn board. They played this under the park shelter so it worked well when the afternoon sun got too hot. I don't know the rules of the game or who invented it, but they all loved playing it. Finding a suitable cap in the gutter became cause for much rejoicing. As I write, I realize this could be more fuel for reporters—it's probably an inner-city game.

Mix It Up, Make It Nice

They played tennis mostly on the weekends when Tom came to the park with us. After he and I played, we would spend a lot of time showing our boys the right way to hit a tennis ball. We enjoyed the game and we wanted it to become a part of their lives, too. We never envisioned it as a potential career.

At this point the rivalry between Thomas and James had not yet developed, but James's mission to emulate his brother in everything had. James accepted that Thomas, three years older and much bigger and stronger than he, could accomplish more. In the only video we have of them playing tennis at this age, we see Thomas showing how well he can hit forehands and backhands and bowing to the camera after he hits an overhead.

When the camera turns on James, perhaps aware of the act he is following, he prefaces his playing with "This won't be very good." In this video James hits with my racket. For some reason, we never thought of buying them junior rackets. More evidence of our parsimony? I don't think so. Tennis was just something they tried their hands at because they saw we enjoyed it. It never occurred to us to invest money in equipment for them. That came later. Until they began to take it seriously, they used whatever was available.

During the years in Yonkers Thomas started kindergarten at the same school his half-brother Chris had attended. The same teacher, Miss Hoehn, was still there. I admired her then and was happy to leave Thomas in her capable hands. When it came time for him to go into first grade, several parents advised me to leave him back since his birthday is two days before the end of the year. Apparently the yardstick for boys was if their birthday fell in September or later they should remain in the lower grade. I asked Miss Hoehn what she thought and she assured me Thomas was exceedingly mature for his age. One of her reasons for this assessment: "He laughs at my jokes."

We sent Thomas to St. Margaret's school in Riverdale because at that time the Yonkers schools had a poor reputation. In the four and a half years he attended the school he never missed a day. At the end of each year he received a "Perfect Attendance" certificate. Minor ailments didn't impress his father. If school was in session, his boys went. This school never closed for snow emergencies since the teachers mostly lived on grounds. I remember bundling James into his stroller and Thomas and I picking our way through the drifts to get him to school.

James attended a head start program before he was old enough for kindergarten. He must have taken a test there because I received a phone call telling me he had qualified for a new program for gifted children called PEARLS. Although it was held in a school on the other end of town, Tom (always high on education) insisted he attend. Thomas came with me on his first day, for his school started later. We assumed, since it was kindergarten, he would only go for half a day. When I realized he had to stay all day, I was anxious about how James would react (he already showed signs of having quite a temper), so I sent Thomas into the class with the lunch we had to buy for him. However it turned out to be such an excellent program that James enjoyed it. He spent one and a half years in PEARLS and it gave him a good foundation for his transfer to public school in Fairfield.

We spent six and a half idyllic years in the house in Yonkers. Since coming to the USA, I had longed to live in my own house again. After more than 20 years I finally realized that dream. Though I was now in my forties, I thoroughly enjoyed my role as mother and homemaker again. The happiest times of my life have been when I had a baby to take care of, and now I had two, as well as a wonderful husband. I find it difficult to imagine anyone choosing a career over motherhood, at least before her children start school. This time goes so quickly and it can never be replaced. I also believe infants and young children have the greatest need for their parents' attention. However I realize not everyone feels the same, and perhaps some will not understand trading pablum for a paycheck.

Mix It Up, Make It Nice

In 1986 Tom's territory changed to cover from New York City to Hartford, so we looked for a place equidistant from both and happily settled on Fairfield Connecticut.

We're all one in the sight of God.

—GLADYS MISSELDINE (my mother)

Chapter 3:
The Armory—Where Tennis Begins

TOM AND I SPENT some of our happiest times playing tennis at the 369th Armory on 134th Street in New York City, and it remained a special place for us even after we moved to Connecticut. It also played an important part in our boys' tennis careers, although we didn't realize this at the time for we had no thoughts of their playing tennis for a living. Certainly, Tom wanted his boys to become professional men, but tennis didn't appear on his list of possible choices.

Many people regard tennis as a summer sport like baseball and softball. Unlike baseball players who seem happy to take a break during the cold-weather months, real tennis aficionados try to play all year 'round. Before the advent of indoor tennis this presented a problem, especially in New England where winters can be long and harsh. In our quest to stretch the season we would sweep snow off the courts, chip away at patches of ice and even purchase our own nets to use when the recreation department stored theirs for the winter. We wore thermals under our warm-ups, knitted hats and gloves with the fingers cut out. Even so, we often had to abandon our efforts for one or two months and wait until the spring thaw in March—that is, until someone thought of indoor tennis. Many of us paid the exorbitant cost just for the thrill of playing our favorite game in January or February when foot-deep snowdrifts covered the courts. Most of us could afford only one game per week and few entertained the thought of playing singles.

As the idea of indoor tennis caught on and more and more facilities opened, we thought the price might come down. In fact it became more expensive, as club owners stretched their seasons to include September and May— ideal times to play tennis outdoors—and insisted on payment for the entire season.

Tom discovered Bill's Indoor Tennis at the 369th Armory through a rabbi who told his mother about it. She worked for him and must have mentioned her son had taken up tennis and was looking for more places to play. The Armory turned out to be the most inexpensive place, for you didn't have to commit for the whole season. You just called and booked a court, and with the reasonable prices at Bill's we often did play singles.

Bill Brown and Claude Cargill ran the Armory at that time. Both warm, friendly people, they soon became our firm friends. Although I know little about their backgrounds, I do know they were dedicated to tennis and to bringing it to underprivileged inner-city children, as well as to providing indoor tennis at reasonable rates for adults. Tom invested in a weekly lesson with Bill, who became his first formal teacher. Claude spent most of his time keeping the junior clinics in line, championing their cause when the city took over the Armory for the homeless. He managed to procure four of the eight courts for the children to use during the day, thus keeping them off the streets. For this, he earned the title "Angel of Harlem."

Tom had been playing at the Armory for some time before he took me there. I went with some misgivings, not knowing what kind of reception I would get for few white people played there. I had no cause to worry. Tom had become a favorite and they all welcomed me as his friend—and as soon as I got used to the fast bounce off the wooden floor, they respected me for my tennis. I found I could compete with the best women players and could hold my own with many of the men.

The Armory's forbidding red brick exterior belies the warmth of its interior. For us it became much more than a place to play tennis. It offered a home away from home. We felt we belonged to a large, loving family—a feeling that persists to this day. We first took Thomas there as an infant in his bassinette. We would park him in the front row of seats where we could keep an eye on him while we played. I recall seeing him raise his head, survey the scene and go back to sleep. Perhaps the sound of bouncing balls had a lulling effect. Three years later, we brought James along to join the family. When they were too young to play with the other children, we needed a volunteer to watch them while we played. We never had to look far. Everyone seemed to love our boys, a feeling that increased as they grew older, and then turned into the admiration they enjoy today.

You entered the Armory through its massive front door, and then proceeded down several long hallways adorned with portraits of long-dead military heroes. Finally you reached the drill hall housing eight temporary tennis courts. (Temporary, because periodically the army would take over and use the space for its intended purpose.) These hallways and the empty rooms and open spaces leading off them made the Armory a children's paradise. They could whoop and holler around the halls with no one to shush them, their lively imaginations creating endless games that all joined in.

Mix It Up, Make It Nice

Tom and I took Thomas and James there every weekend, a practice that continued after we moved from Yonkers. "Our only reason for bringing them to the courts with us was so we could be together," Tom explained to an interviewer many years later. I don't believe, as James often maintains, we were too cheap to hire a babysitter. Actually, that option never occurred to us. A close family, we enjoyed having our children with us. Whatever the reason, as our kids grew older they had fun with the children whose parents also chose not to hire a babysitter. When they tired of games in the hallway, they would sometimes get on the court and try their hands with a racket. They enjoyed playing, but both admit today they couldn't wait to get back to the games in the hall.

Coming into the Armory from the cold, you immediately felt the warmth, not just the temperature but also the whole atmosphere. As you drew closer to the courts, the fragrance of coffee brewing, often mingled with mixed aromas of food being heated, would greet you from the kitchen just off the drill hall. Not the kind of club where you played your hour and a half and left, players at the Armory would come prepared to stay most of the day. Along with their rackets, women brought their knitting or crocheting. Between games, we ladies would sit in the stands, comparing patterns and progress from one week to the next. Behind the backcourts, men played or watched chess when they took a break from playing tennis. The place constantly hummed with activity and laughter.

As soon as our boys could handle a racket, they wanted to try to hit some balls. Always wanting to emulate his big brother, James began at a younger age than Thomas. With Thomas in nursery school I would take James, aged 2-1/2, with me if I played at the Armory during the week. One lady, Hannah Czywinski, paid for the court time and then paid me to hit balls to her. Even though this was gainful employment, I still never thought of leaving James with a babysitter. Hannah actually wanted James to come along. She had seen him at Fay Park and he impressed her. Five minutes before the hour ended she invited him onto the court. After amusing

The Armory—Where Tennis Begins

himself in the stands for 55 minutes, James welcomed the opportunity for action. He and I would stand on opposite service lines, he with my mid-size Yonex, and hit balls back and forth across the net. He amazed Hannah with his control; prompting her to remark "He's going to be something some day." I have long since lost touch with her, but I often wonder if she realizes how prophetic were her words.

This idyllic situation ended abruptly in 1985 when, with no warning, the city took over the Armory to shelter homeless men. Though devastated by the loss of our winter recreation, we had to concede tennis is just a game, and we couldn't justify playing while someone might be freezing to death. For the children it had meant more than recreation. The Armory had provided an after-school haven, an alternative to the streets. Claude Cargill, co-proprietor of the club, feared for the fate of the many children who now would have nowhere to go when school ended. He pleaded for some way to continue his junior programs and before long he got his wish. The city allowed him to use half of the floor during the day when many of the homeless went out, but at night it had to convert back to a dormitory.

Although we adults couldn't play, we still took the boys to the Armory on weekends. Now 5 and very good for his age, James played in the program, too, but before anyone could play we had work to do. We folded and stacked cots, cleaned the vast floor of cigarette butts, food wrappers, tissues and myriad other more objectionable items, laid and carefully smoothed out the rubber carpet, positioned eight posts and strung up four nets. Everyone helped— parents, kids, coaches—and before long scores of children were swinging their rackets to the accompaniment of blaring music, sporadic outbursts of fighting, and ribald or sarcastic comments from men peeking around the dividing curtain—a far cry from the waving palms and glistening turquoise waters that provide the backdrop for most of today's seriously aspiring young tennis players. For us it was not so serious. "It was just something we enjoyed and we hoped it would be something they could enjoy for the rest of their lives," Tom recalled later to another interviewer.

Eventually the homeless moved out and we had our tennis courts back again. Now the proprietors invested in permanent rubberized flooring, which made the game much better. Tom would often stop in after working in the city, and, during the winter months, I became resigned to late suppers. As a family, we spent most of our weekends there. The Armory provided not only recreation but it became part of our social life too. Luckily, we both had simple tastes and always seemed to agree on what to do with our leisure time. Tom and I belonged to various leagues and often entered tournaments, both singles and mixed doubles. We never argued the way many other couples did. He believed encouragement produced better results than censure, a technique we employed with our sons when they began more serious competition.

An excerpt from an interview James gave in 1998 illustrates how much easier it is to play without pressure. "I've talked to a bunch of guys who have told me horror stories about guys they're playing doubles with, yelling at them during the match, blaming them. I've played horrible matches with my brother and no matter what, the next point we'll laugh about it. He'll say, 'Hey, it's my fault, don't worry about it.' I know in my heart there's no way it was his fault, he's just helping me through it. The fact he does that makes me feel 10 times more comfortable." This is exactly the way Tom and I played doubles together, and reading that made us feel good it had rubbed off on them.

We entered our boys whenever they held junior tournaments at the Armory. I don't recall any spectacular results, but we felt they benefited from the competition, and they learned about winning and losing at an early age. Thomas and James developed their own individual ways to handle losses. A very young Thomas once lost a close match in a tournament at the Armory and then disappeared. We searched all over for him and finally found him crying in the uppermost rows of seats. Fortunately he seemed to come to grips with it early and though I know he felt subsequent losses deeply, he would always assure me it didn't matter—it wasn't important. James reacted differently. The problem started later with him, for during those early years at the Armory he just seemed happy to swing a racket and felt gratified in the way he always made contact. When the competition became more serious, however, he put more and more pressure on himself.

During their teens, when our boys became more involved in junior tennis in New England and finally began to do well, they didn't need the free clinics at the Armory any more. Tom and I still played there on weekends when we weren't driving to a New England junior tournament. The boys stayed in contact by helping out with the clinics and with the homework club. (To stay in the program a student must maintain at least a C average.) James told a reporter, "I try to get down every other Saturday to volunteer. I teach a little or help with the homework club. It's just kind of to show them that where they are, I was, maybe 10 or 11 years ago. So you can still do something positive when you're coming from there."

L ONG BEFORE I MET Tom I had often pondered the racial situation in this country, especially during the three years I lived in Missouri in the '50s, where blatant racism still existed. I had never encountered this in England. Tom and I discussed it frequently, and although he made me see it in a new light, yet I believe as a Caucasian I can never empathize entirely with the plight of an African American in this country.

I came closest to an understanding one Saturday afternoon. I had a part-time job in recreation at a children's home in Yonkers. A Black counselor and I took a group of teenagers to New York City for the day. Our last stop was a movie. The film had no visible redeeming qualities—soap-opera dialogue, contrived scenes, bad acting—it seemed to have been made expressly to incite racial strife. Near the end, the Black hero set the white villain on fire. Excitement in the audience rose to fever pitch. One girl near me stood up, shook her fist at the screen and yelled, "Now you're Black like me."

Mix It Up, Make It Nice

As the noise intensified, I sank lower and lower into my seat, wondering what would happen when the lights went on. Stuck in the middle of a row, I couldn't even take refuge in the ladies' room. Harold, the other counselor, realized my plight. As soon as the movie ended, he hustled the girls back to the van for the ride home. Immensely uncomfortable, I sat in the back with the girls. I gazed out the window trying to look unconcerned, but with my thoughts racing. Should I attempt to discuss this with them—try to point out the film's obvious flaws and its crass exploitation of race relations? Should I keep quiet and hope they would soon forget it? Suddenly I sensed trouble. The van had become eerily quiet. I looked around and saw one girl with a lighter in her hand, advancing the flame towards me, seemingly intent on recreating the movie's last scene. I held my breath. I couldn't think what to say or do. Luckily, Harold, glancing in the rear view mirror, took in the situation. "Put that out, Rose," he insisted. After what seemed an eternity, Rose obeyed. Everyone, including me, breathed again.

The rest of the ride proved uneventful. I couldn't wait for it to end. Looking for sympathy and feeling hugely sorry for myself, I sought out a friend the next day. Father Stuart Sandberg listened patiently to my sad story, then, instead of the comfort I had sought, he observed, "Well, now you know how it feels."

Do I really know how it feels? I caught just a glimpse of it that day. How do you live with that feeling every day of your life? That must be what Arthur Ashe meant when he said despite all the other burdens he had to bear, especially towards the end of his life, being Black was the greatest.

Both Thomas and James have been victims of profiling here in Connecticut. They tended to downplay it, but their father and I knew better. I could drive my car for a year or more with an expired emissions sticker. If one of them drove it for a day, I knew I would have to take care of that piece of business. When it happened to Thomas, I thought maybe it was an isolated case. A few years later, James drove my car and I joked with him at least no one had bothered him about the emissions sticker (out of date again). "Sorry, Mom," he said. "Check your glove compartment." He had received a warning. I once had a Saab that informed me if a headlight or a brake light failed. When Thomas saw that on the dashboard, he refused to drive my car. Yet no one ever bothered me about it. I find it interesting their problems on this score happen only with people who don't know them. In school they were extremely well-liked and popular with their fellow students, as well as their teachers—which points up exactly what prejudice is: judging someone solely on the basis of their outward appearance.

James encountered racism at the US Open in 2001. In the third set, Lleyton Hewitt, having lost one set to James and in danger of losing another, pointed out to the umpire the similarity between James's skin color and that of the linesman who had called him twice for foot faults. He demanded the linesman be removed. At one of the ensuing press conferences when reporters waited to see how James would handle it, one of his comments was, "My parents have been through a lot more than I have." Yes, the situation is certainly getting better but racism is still alive and well, as any Black person will tell you. We can legislate against it, but how do you eradicate it from the heart? Some parents still bring up their children to look on different races as inferior, and what you learn as a child tends to stay with you. My mom always maintained, "We're all one in the sight of God." A pity she couldn't raise all of God's children.

We will never achieve racial harmony anywhere in the world until we all can look at people as just people. In Tony Hendra's book *Father Joe: The Man Who Saved My Soul* he says, "There weren't two kinds of people in the world for Joe, nor three, nor ten. Just people." Father Joe possessed a unique perspective on life. Unfortunately, few of us are able to feel this way, and fewer still can act on it.

I believe my oldest son Howard has achieved this. Now the headmaster at an elementary school in New Jersey where most of the students belong to minority groups, he treats all students only on their merits. This attitude started long ago. As a student at Yonkers High School, I recall someone commenting to him the school had a lot of "nightfighters" in its student body. "I don't know, I never noticed," came the perfect answer. Knowing Howard, it wasn't meant to be a put-down—just a statement of fact.

Through Tom, I have associated so much with Black people I feel comfortable judging them as just people. Once, when the captain of my USTA team told me a certain lady had joined the team, I told her immediately and vehemently I never wanted to play as her partner. I didn't understand the horrified look I received until it dawned on me the lady in question was Black, and the captain probably judged this a racist remark. I had encountered this lady in various tournaments and had decided she was not the kind of person with whom I wanted to associate, and my decision had nothing to do with her complexion. To me she was just a person, not a Black person. To prove their tolerance people often say, "Some of my best friends are Black (Jewish, etc.). I feel it would mean more if we could say, "Some of my enemies are Black." We need to judge people for their actions, not their looks.

In his book *I Never Had It Made*, Jackie Robinson bemoans the fact when he first broke the color barrier he couldn't be himself. He had to be squeaky clean or he would be condemned, and he was picked on even when he was squeaky clean. This is what Tom realized when he imposed an early curfew on our boys. "If there's trouble, who will the police pick on first?" he asked, and he didn't mean because Thomas stood a head taller than most of his friends. It shouldn't have to be this way, but unfortunately, even though we congratulate ourselves we have come a long way, this attitude lingers still.

In yet another incident, one day Tom and I were playing tennis at some courts in Yonkers. I came off the courts while he stayed on to play longer. All the seats around the courts had one or two people sitting on them. Without thinking, I sat down next to a young Black girl. Later, when Tom came off the courts, he looked at me, his eyes shining, and told me how good it made him feel to see me sit there. I had done it without thinking, but he had noticed it. To a Black person in our society, race is always present.

We tend to feel complacent about the present race situation, but just 30 years ago Tom and I were harassed several times by pornographic hate mail, and it's less than 10 years since we appealed to the FBI after we both received threatening letters at our places of business. After that, a policeman came around periodically to make sure no one had made good on the threats—this in Fairfield Connecticut in the late '90s. I could tell many more stories on this subject, but I think you get the picture.

The Armory remained an important part of our lives for so long it's difficult for me to remember all the details. I wish Tom were here to help me. Even in his last year with us, he would stop in at the Armory several times each week. He could no longer play tennis, but his mind stayed sharp and he enjoyed playing or watching the chess games and just being a part of that warm, loving atmosphere.

After Thomas and James turned pro, they still wanted to give back to the Armory. Every year around Christmas they put on an exhibition. They conduct a clinic in which they hit balls with all of the current clinic participants, they hold a forum where they answer whatever questions the children and parents put to them and they sign endless autographs. Although the outward aspect of the Armory has changed drastically, many of the people we knew are still there. When I return to the Armory to watch the exhibition, I get hugs and kisses all around. We're still part of the family.

*Thomas and James with the Harlem clinic
at their annual exhibition.*

*John McEnroe, James, Dante Brown and Thomas
at the Harlem Exhibition.*

*One of the luckiest things that can happen to you
in life is, I think, to have a happy childhood.*

—AGATHA CHRISTIE

Chapter 4:
Childhood in Connecticut

WE MOVED TO FAIRFIELD Connecticut in January 1986 on a frigid, gray Saturday. Both our boys had become popular at their respective schools and felt the hurt of leaving a familiar, comfortable situation for the unknown. That first weekend proved bleak and seemed endless. Although busy with unpacking and making the house habitable, I couldn't fail to notice Thomas and James went through the weekend looking as if they had lost their best friends, which, in fact, they had. I began to feel guilty for uprooting them.

On Monday morning they both went to Stratfield School; Thomas to fourth grade and James to first. I spent the day worrying about what kind of reception they would get. They came home together on the school bus, and before I could query them about their first day in school, the doorbell rang. About a half-dozen boys ringed the front steps asking whether Thomas could come out and play. I felt like hugging every one of them. Of course, James tagged along.

I soon realized while the neighborhood teemed with boys the same age as Thomas, there were no younger children for James to play with. I have often felt this played a large part in the development of his work ethic and ultimately his career. He and Thomas always went out to play together, so James had to compete with boys three and four years older. While Thomas held his own easily with his peers, James always had to put forth his best effort to stay close. I realize now it was quite extraordinary he could stay close, but at the time I was just happy the other boys accepted him.

James had always looked up to Thomas, but now he began to compete with him, and this proved a source of great frustration for a long period of his childhood. While he could compete with many of the older boys—Thomas's friends—he could never seem to get the better of his brother. In athletic endeavors, in board games, in Nintendo games, even when luck was the only factor, James could never seem to win. Thomas always gloated over his wins, annoying James even more. I suffered his frustration with him, and would sometimes offer up a silent prayer to please let James win just one game. Perhaps the Almighty had different plans, and could see much further down the road.

In sixth grade Thomas became one of a select group chosen to take an enrichment science course at Talcott Mountain in Avon. When James got to sixth grade and was selected for the same group, he was ecstatic. His esteem for his big brother almost amounted to hero-worship, and he wanted to follow in his footsteps. Thomas also excelled at math, and his teachers always put him in the highest group. In middle school they initially placed James in a lower group. When they decided he belonged in the top group, he came home bubbling over with the news.

He had to work much harder than his brother to maintain the position, but he didn't seem to mind.

Despite his admiration for Thomas, James's temper often flared up in the constant battles they had, sometimes almost driving me to distraction. Their father, one of four sons, advised me to try to ignore it, assuring me they would work it out themselves. As always, he was right.

Not long after we moved, Tom came up with a plan to motivate them to read more. Thomas needed little motivation. As soon as he learned to read he devoured books of all descriptions, but James needed a push. They had to list each book they read, and when they reached 100 they earned $25. Tom kept those lists, and I found them when I cleaned out his office. They cover a lengthy span of time. James's list starts with such books as Dr. Seuss's *Green Eggs and Ham* and *Hop on Pop* entered in a childish print, and continues in cursive writing with more mature books. Thomas often read much longer books than James, and suggested to his father such works as Dickens's *Great Expectations* should warrant at least two points. His father agreed.

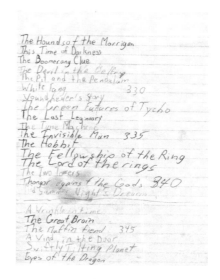

A page from Thomas's reading list.

Tom hadn't discovered the joy of reading until he reached adulthood. When I met him, he always carried a book with him, trying to make up for lost time. He loved to see me read to our sons. I would sit one on each knee and read until one of them had enough, or until bedtime intervened. I recall looking up one day and seeing Tom gazing at us, his eyes shining. Until that day I hadn't realized how much he valued it. To me, it was just something one did. My mother read to us, so I read to my children. Unfortunately, I find not all children are so blessed. If more parents would try it, they would realize it benefits not only their children, it also provides a wonderful way to bond with them. There's also a lot of wisdom in children's books, most particularly those by Dr. Seuss. We could learn a lot from such stories as *The Sneetches*, *Yertle the Turtle*, *Horton Hears a Who*, and, of course, *How the Grinch Stole Christmas*. There could be a lot more harmony and happiness in the world if we espoused the values in these books.

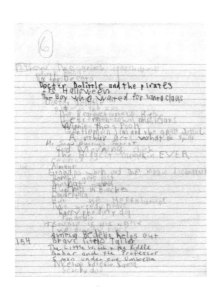

A page from James's reading list.

One still stands out in my memory—*Too Many Daves*, a Doctor Seuss story about a woman with 23 children whom she all called by the same name, Dave. It then lists some names she wished she had used, some quite normal, others completely ridiculous. I'll never forget how much fun we had with that story; I had to stop reading for a while until we all stopped laughing.

Although it made me happy when they both learned to read for themselves, I missed having them sit on my knees with my arms around them. Later, I would read to them while they ate dinner. Among others, I recall reading *Animal Farm* and *A Midsummer Night's Dream*. Both led to lively discussions.

As the boys grew older, Tom delegated certain daily chores. They had to wash and dry the dishes and take out the garbage. Once a week they helped clean the house. Though they agitated for it, Tom didn't believe in giving pocket money for this, so besides the reading they looked for other ways to earn money. They found they could deliver papers in Fairfield before age 12 (the minimum age in Yonkers). For several years they shared a neighborhood route after school. James always took longer to deliver his papers because he stopped to befriend all the dogs and cats in the area. Later on, this love for animals became another source of revenue. James initiated his own pet service. "You leave 'em, I love 'em," announced the flier he dropped into neighbors' mailboxes. He acquired several regular customers whose dogs became so used to our house their owners still called me after James left for college. I had become fond of the animals too (with the possible exception of Ashley), so I took them in rather than have them sent to a kennel. I mentioned this to James and he, ever the entrepreneur, suggested if they paid me he should get a 5 percent finder's fee. That didn't happen.

I had misgivings about Ashley as soon as she came into the house, and insisted James walk her often. Apparently he didn't walk her often enough. On the second day of Ashley's stay, I came home from work, took off my sneakers and socks, made a cup of tea and prepared to relax. Before I reached the armchair with my mug and my book, I found myself ankle deep in about five pounds of a particularly squishy Ashley accident.

"James," I hollered, afraid to move. My tone of voice made him react immediately. He stopped dead at the doorway, taking in the scene.

"Don't stand there," I said. "Get me some paper towels—lots of them."

Gingerly, I extricated my feet and started cleaning up, while James, carefully keeping his distance, sprayed the room liberally with air freshener. I made him walk Ashley again, although after what I had just dealt with it seemed an unnecessary endeavor. With Ashley out of the way, our cat crept in, looking around warily.

"Poor puss," I thought. "She's had a rough time with that dog here. I'll give her a treat."

Mix It Up, Make It Nice

I opened a can of her favorite mackerel and dumped it all into her dish. Then I put my feet in the sink to finish the cleanup. A little sweet-smelling talcum, and I settled again with my book and my now tepid cup of tea. The cat, done with her treat, followed me in and promptly threw up on Thomas's recently purchased yearbook (a steal at $75), which he had left on the floor.

At this point James returned with his charge.

"Your turn to clean up," I said, indicating the mess on the floor.

"No way," he said. "I'm taking care of Ashley. She's your cat."

Ashley didn't visit again.

At different times of the year they found other ways to earn money. They would shovel snow, rake leaves, mow lawns and even baby-sit for the neighbors. James briefly became an altar boy, but I suspect the motivation was the annual trip to an amusement park and the tips he received at weddings and funerals rather than any religious fervor. Small for his age, James, with his softly curling hair, had an angelic look about him, which became enhanced by his altar-boy vestments. Because of this, he was in demand for special religious occasions.

But what about tennis? January turned out to be a bad time to relocate. We couldn't play outdoors, and by that time everyone had their indoor tennis scheduled. The homeless still occupied the Armory in Harlem, so we couldn't play on weekends except in the junior clinics. Desperate for exercise, I took up jogging every morning before waking Thomas and James for school, so tennis took a back seat for a while.

I don't remember when Thomas and James began playing tennis in Fairfield. We must have taken them with us to the courts during that first summer—still too cheap to hire a sitter. We visited several indoor courts for tryouts. At one club the head pro set up his hopper on the service line and tossed a ball to James (6 years old and small for his age). After James hit a few forehands past him, he picked up the hopper and moved to the baseline.

Childhood in Connecticut

He instantly became interested in our boys and invited us to play on his private court. They enjoyed that outing, mainly because he let them use his swimming pool and when fall came we enrolled them in one of his club clinics.

In an effort to find more tennis players, Tom and I entered the town tournament. Tom became friendly with one of his opponents, a man named Tim Steers. They chatted after they played, and Tim told Tom about The Tennis Club of Trumbull, which his son, John, attended. We took our boys there and they hit for a while with the owner, Ed Pagano. He recognized Thomas and James had some potential, and he began to nurture their talent. A laid-back individual, Ed had trouble dealing with James's temper, and soon suggested they work with his head pro, Brian Barker. Thus began a long and enduring relationship.

Over many years, Brian has become much more than a tennis coach—mentor, friend, adviser, a shoulder to cry on, almost one of the family. When we first met him in 1987, he was in charge of the junior tennis program at The Tennis Club of Trumbull. He had taken up tennis at age 11, after baseball no longer presented a challenge. He took his first tennis lessons at the Trumbull Racquet Club with Ed Pagano, who later started his own club—The Tennis Club of Trumbull. Brian learned fast, and before long had qualified to play on a national level. He posted an outstanding high school tennis record (he lost one match in four years), and then went on to play for the University of South Carolina. After graduation, Brian tried his luck on the pro circuit. He had some modest triumphs, reaching as high as 646 in the pro ranks. But he was not impressed with the life led by a player in the minor leagues of tennis, and later confessed to me how relieved he felt when he decided to quit. He then began doing what he does best—coaching and counseling young tennis players.

At first we invested in a half-hour shared lesson with Brian. Thomas took the first 20 minutes and James finished the half hour. A few years later we felt their progress warranted a half hour each. By this time James had begun to develop a temper, and his lesson often consisted of five minutes of hitting and 25 minutes sitting on the bench discussing his attitude. James realizes now those lectures played an important part in his development, but at the time it was difficult for anyone to get through to him. One day, Ed, on an adjacent court, witnessed a particularly nerve-wracking rant by James. Brian, a man of few words, remarked to his complacently smiling boss, "Thanks a lot, Ed."

Another time, much later on, I saw a mother watching her son take his first lesson with Brian. Brian and his new player stood at the net talking at length. As James and I walked by, I commented to James the mother looked a little unhappy. Apparently she expected more for her money than a lecture. "She doesn't realize it," said James, "but those talks can be much more important than hitting balls. I didn't see it then, but I can now." But until he did see it, he made a lot of lives miserable.

When they began playing in clinics with others at the club, James's temper sometimes became ugly. Recognizing his talent, Brian would feed more difficult balls to him to give others in the group a chance to win. At that time James (like Vince Lombardi) believed winning was the only thing, and he couldn't tolerate the injustice of it. He called Brian a jerk.

Brian didn't feel he should have to put up with this behavior. He appealed to Tom and me and suggested James take a long break from tennis to try to calm him down.

"He's got the talent," he told us, "And he's young enough that it won't hurt him to take a year off."

Tom wouldn't hear of it.

"We'll work through it," he resolved; and work through it we did. It wasn't easy. Sometimes James's attitude made me feel like banging my head against a wall. He would get furious when he missed a shot—any shot. I tried to tell him sometimes you just have to acknowledge your opponent hit a winner, applaud it and go on to the next point. He didn't believe it—nothing should beat him. Now, when I watch him play and see him compliment his opponent on a good shot, or applaud by clapping his left hand on his racket strings, my words come back to me. From being the worst tennis brat James has become known as one of the best sports in the game. I remember an English writer's comment after James played Mariano Zabaleta, one of his first matches at Wimbledon. He claimed not only was James outplaying his opponent, he was "outnicing" him too. In those early days I would never have believed this could happen.

As the boys improved, Brian suggested practicing before school and before the club officially opened, as an inexpensive way to get more court time. It started when Thomas was a freshman in high school. He had quickly taken over the number-one singles spot, and Brian offered to work with him and any other members of the team who felt like getting up early. Either Tom or I would abandon our cozy flannel sheets at 5:30, drive Thomas to the courts and then make sure he got to school by 7:30. Sometimes James opted to come too, and then we all went. James would have liked to hit with the older boys, but he had to settle for playing with Tom and me on an empty court. This did wonders for his game, for Tom would patiently instruct him in the correct strokes.

By the time James started high school, Thomas had his driver's license so there was no need for us all to go, but we had come to enjoy spending this extra time together, and while they worked with Brian, Tom and I drilled on an empty court. On several frosty mornings each week we would all cram into Thomas's second-hand Celica (an early graduation gift, given with the assurance from him he would end the year with at least a 4.0 average—he did). Thomas drove, with Tom in the passenger seat and James and I huddled on the inadequate back seat, our heads leaning towards each other because the roof was so low, sharing a cup of tea and wishing the heat would reach us.

They would all hit for an hour and a half, Brian feeding balls to them, his parka buttoned to the neck with the collar turned up, for there was no heat at that hour. While they showered, I prepared their breakfast, a microwaved bagel, a carton of Tropicana and usually a shared bag of popcorn, which they ate on the way to school while Tom now took care of the driving. We left them and the car at the high school, and Tom and I walked home to begin our day.

The car James drove in high school—formerly his brother Thomas's graduation gift.

These early sessions with Brian at The Tennis Club of Trumbull led to a major change in my life. One morning when we came up from the courts, I found the baby-sitter behind the desk. She told me Ed, the owner, was having trouble finding people to open up in the mornings, so she had been helping out by doing it twice a week. She asked me if I would be interested in manning the desk on the mornings I was there. We always arrived before the club opened, so I was already there when the first customers came in. I consulted Tom, and, as always, he left it up to me.

At the time, I was working in the Continuing Education Department at Fairfield University. When we moved to Fairfield, with the boys still so young, I looked for work close to home. The first two positions didn't work out, but then I applied to Sacred Heart University, and found, not only a position I enjoyed, but also the means to realize a long-time dream.

One of my co-workers told me employees could take university courses free of charge. Learning has always appealed to me, and before my first marriage I had earned 60 credits towards a Bachelor's degree in Fine Arts. Excited at the prospect of continuing after a lengthy interruption, I called my sister who still lived in Jefferson City Missouri, where I had attended Jefferson City Junior College. She found my transcript, and Sacred Heart accepted the credits. I couldn't wait to get started.

Everything seemed rosy. I enjoyed working as the dean's secretary, and I enjoyed even more the evening classes I took. Then the administration saw fit to eliminate that particular dean's position, and although he gave me glowing references, they couldn't find a suitable place for me. Devastated at the thought of abandoning my studies, I called Fairfield University.

"Do you give free tuition to your employees?" I asked.

"We do."

"Do you have a job for me?"

They placed me in the Continuing Education Department, where the dean soon realized I had a talent for picking up errors. I became the proofreader for their many brochures, and eventually for the Continuing Education catalogue. I also took care of arranging the art trips abroad, as well as running the Institute for Retired Professionals, all of which I enjoyed immensely.

Almost immediately I resumed my studies. The dean intimated they would offer me a more prestigious position as soon as I graduated, so I worked even harder. I took lunchtime courses and summer classes; I even used my vacation time to take a one-week intensive course.

The hard work paid off, and in 1992 at the untraditional age of 56, I graduated *summa cum laude*, with a bachelor's degree in English Literature and Writing from Fairfield University. I felt a tremendous sense of accomplishment. I had wanted to do this since I left Missouri in 1954.

Graduation day, May 1992.

After graduation, I began working on some credits toward a master's degree. A position of more responsibility arose in our department, and I reminded the dean of his promise. He gave the position to a new applicant, a young lady who proved less qualified than I. At this point, I asked Thomas and James if they would consider attending Fairfield University, for they could get free tuition if I stayed there. After an emphatic "No Way!" from both of them, I began thinking about leaving my *alma mater*.

The opportunity to spend more time at the tennis club appealed to me. For a time I worked there two mornings each week, from 6:30 until 8:30, then left for the university. I learned the work quickly, and before long Ed asked me if I would consider longer hours. With the deteriorating situation at the university, the idea appealed to me. Again I consulted Tom. As usual, he wanted me to do anything that would make me happy, even though I wouldn't be able to contribute as much to the household expenses. With a big smile on his face he assured me we would be able to make it. At the beginning of July 1993, I handed the dean my resignation.

I began working a four-hour shift for a few days each week. In no time, it developed into four hours for five days and six hours on Sundays. At some point, I filled in for a missing pro in one of the junior clinics. That led eventually to having my own clinics to teach on Saturdays. I was at the club every day of the week, but now going to work seemed more like play. I loved the atmosphere of a tennis club, and with Thomas and James coming in for clinics several times a week, it meant spending more time with them and watching their progress. In addition, as an employee I could get free court time, so I would often play for an hour or more before my shift began at 10:30.

Among all these pluses, the one that topped them all was meeting Erika Ceccarelli, who has become my best friend. At the time I began at the club, Erika worked the shift after mine, 2:30 until 6:30. I would often stay after my shift ended so she could help me to understand the intricate workings of an indoor tennis club. On Mondays and Wednesdays Thomas and James came in for their clinic, so I stayed even longer to watch them play.

Erika came to this country from Nuremberg Germany in her early twenties, so right away our European backgrounds gave us plenty to talk about. We found that schools in our respective countries are quite similar, and we discussed our school days at length. An intelligent lady, I often marvel at Erika's command of the English language, as well as her drive to augment it. If I use a word with which she is unfamiliar, she asks me its meaning, writes it down, then tries to use it.

Erika had met her husband Bob after World War II, when he was stationed in Germany. He brought her to this country, where they married and are the parents of five children. At the time I met Erika, she was experiencing a huge crisis in her life. While in college her oldest daughter Sabina had been diagnosed with a rare form of cancer for which there is as yet no cure. As Sabina's situation worsened, Erika's devotion to her every need increased. At that time she worked only three days each week at the club, and I'm sure she only worked at all because Sabina insisted on her having some life of her own. Erika never worked during the summer, because her daughter enjoyed sitting by a neighbor's pool or going to the beach.

At age 29, Sabina lost her battle with cancer. Although she knew it was inevitable, Erika was overcome with grief. After Sabina's death, Erika began to spend more time at the club, and our friendship deepened and gradually became what it is today.

When Erika felt ready to come back to work, it proved a big help in assuaging her grief. By this time Ed had put me in charge of making up the shift schedule. I soon realized working was therapy for Erika—"When I'm here, I laugh. When I'm home, I cry," she had said one day. I convinced Ed it would be good policy to have some continuity in the schedule, with me always there in the morning, and now to have Erika there every afternoon. She agreed to it, as did Ed. She also worked a six-hour shift on Saturday afternoon, so now we both spent a lot of time at the club, and gradually took over more and more responsibilities. Once, when we both took vacations at the same time, Ed, realizing how much he relied on us, made us promise we would never do that again.

In those days, the club was a happy place. I often said it was a sitcom waiting for a writer. Ed rarely acted like a boss, and we could kid with him as much as with our co-workers. No one took offense, and we were all so comfortable with each other we laughed when teased about our shortcomings. We were one big, happy family.

After Thomas left for college, James, too young to drive, had no way to get to the club. Erika's daughter Lara attended the same school as James and was in the same clinic. Erika would pick them both up at 2:00 and get them to the club by 2:30 to begin her shift. Ever the mother, she always brought lunch for them, and sometimes brought a whole bag of bagels for us all to share.

Because it was such a happy place, I often stayed for several hours after my shift ended. As soon as Erika arrived I would put on the kettle and make tea for both of us, which we enjoyed while I told her what had been happening during my shift. Erika and I found we had the same views on many issues, especially on bringing up children, so we always found plenty to talk about, and that still holds true today. She is the most generous person I have ever met. I never feel I can do enough to repay her many kindnesses towards my family and me. For this reason, you will always see Erika sitting next to me in the family box at the US Open. Along with countless other benefits, I'm so grateful to James for making it possible for me to give this to her.

Erika Ceccarelli and me
at The Tennis Club of Trumbull.

OUR HOUSE IN FAIRFIELD falls into the middle-class category—three and a half bedrooms, two bathrooms and a good-sized backyard. It sits in the middle of a quiet block with so little traffic it could qualify as a play street. Each house has a well-manicured front lawn, and the street boasts an abundance of trees. Yet even though an early article in *Sports Illustrated* noted we now live in "one of the wealthiest zip codes in the U.S.," reporters still found grist for their mills. The April 2002 issue of *Connecticut Magazine* felt the need to mention we lived on "a street where the houses sit so close together that the mail carrier still walks door to door." When this article appeared, we had lived in Connecticut for 16 years, yet I had never realized one's method of mail delivery constituted a status symbol, and I certainly don't recall feeling victimized by it.

A more recent piece saw fit to point out James grew up in a house with one bathroom. (He didn't.) Perhaps an over-abundance of bathrooms has also become a status symbol. At the risk of starting up the violins, our family enjoyed a wealth greater than material goods can supply. Harmony pervaded our home, a feeling of mutual respect, love, and, an essential ingredient, humor. Tom and I shared 18 glorious years in our modest house, watching our sons grow, sharing their joys and disappointments. We had fun together, laughing with each other, and often at each other, in the way only those who share a deep love can. We always supplied our children's needs, but not necessarily their wants. I believe this has contributed to their characters, which many people admire. When children are given everything they desire (often to assuage parental guilt), they continually look for more instead of being content with what they have—and this can carry over into adulthood. Philosophers, in their eternal search for happiness, often point to those who feel content with their lot and have no need to look around to see if their neighbor is going them one better.

Probably the most egregious piece of fiction written about James and his family appeared in a magazine called *Departures* in March 2003. Although the reporter drove James home and saw how our three-story house was situated, she still described it as a "modest bungalow outside the dingy industrial smokestacks of Bridgeport." She would have had to drive a long way to see smokestacks, but just around the corner she would have come upon the rather exclusive Brooklawn Country Club, which she chose not to mention. Then the writer verged on the insulting when she asserted, "tennis was his ticket out." Out of what? Fairfield Connecticut? Harvard University? Many would be happy to have a ticket in.

She went on to observe, "most of the family's money went toward tennis"—another fabrication. Tennis was important to us, but only as recreation. It was never a priority. We spent relatively little on lessons. Tennis in Harlem was free because Tom and I volunteered in the program. Their half-hour shared lesson with Brian Barker, James's current and only coach, didn't break the bank. We supplemented it with teaching them ourselves, usually on the free public courts. When they had their own half hour each, it was still well within the budget, and as they grew older and showed some promise, we enrolled them in a tournament training program that met for an hour and a half three times per week at The Tennis Club of Trumbull. Because I worked at the club, the owner let me pay for one child and the other could take part if someone didn't show up, which was often the case for they used all six courts with 24 players enrolled. If all 24 showed up, they split the time between them.

Even when our boys began playing in national tournaments, and some of our friends suggested it, we never considered sending them to a tennis academy, not necessarily because of the expense involved but because it meant school would become secondary. Typically at these academies tennis takes up the first part of the day and schoolwork comes second, when the child is often too tired to concentrate. That instantly doomed the idea for us; also we didn't consider tennis a worthwhile reason to disrupt the family. In contrast, when Thomas received his acceptance letter from Harvard in December 1994, we didn't consider the expense—for that Tom would willingly have mortgaged the house and gone into debt, but with both of us contributing towards the fees, that proved unnecessary.

We did feel justified in paying the costly entrance fees when they began to qualify for national tournaments, because we wanted to find out just how much talent they had, but we only allowed them to enter tournaments that would not interfere with their attendance at school. We

61

wanted to find out how they would fare against the best young players in the country. First results for both boys proved adequate, but certainly not stellar.

In an interview during his last year in high school, James said to play tennis for a living would be a dream come true. At that time though, it was only a dream. In a later interview, he said at age 14 he felt he would be more likely to win the lottery than become a professional tennis player. In 2001, after two years on the pro circuit, he looked back on his junior years and observed, "When I was about 10 years old I probably dreamed I was going to be a pro tennis player. I am also very realistic. When I was 14, 15 years old—not making Nationals—I thought I'd like to be a good college player. I just wanted to work hard and know I did my best. Before you know it, being a good college player was what I had done. I felt like I could still improve. Now I am where I am. I have come pretty far ... I still feel like I can improve."

I think this attitude has a lot to do with the way James feels about his current success. He appreciates he is living a dream life, and has little patience with pros who complain about the condition of the courts, the size of their hotel room and other minor hardships.

Another assertion I objected to in this same article was James suffered because of his mixed heritage. First, the writer talks of James's feelings about having to wear a brace (for scoliosis), making him different from his classmates and of how he just wanted to fit in. Then she claims, "As the child of a white mother and an African American father in Connecticut, that was no simple task." From the first day our boys started school here, they had no problems on that score. Two of the most well-adjusted and well-liked boys in school, both were voted "Parents' Dream Child" in their senior year. Thomas's adviser once told me Thomas is the kid everyone wants to hate, because he goes through his assignments so easily, but you can't hate him because he's so likeable.

The same article pointing out our dearth of bathrooms describes me as a "sharp-featured, sardonic English woman." I attribute the sharp features to my weight loss after Tom's death. I'm finding it hard to gain it back. It's called grief. I realize this comment does sound sardonic, but I believe accounts of our home life such as I have described here invite sardonic comments, which I have trouble stifling. I'm afraid I also wax a little sardonic at the over-abundance of "friends" I seem to have acquired since James has jumped into the public eye. I often have trouble recalling their names.

By Fairfield standards we did live modestly, yet I don't recall ever feeling deprived and our boys had little trouble dealing with it. Sometimes it became difficult, as when one of their friends was rewarded with a new car for bringing his grades from D to C. Thomas had to settle for a used Celica as a reward for maintaining his 4.0 average throughout high school.

Again, I believe this kind of treatment helped shape their characters. I found myself continually counting my blessings, for my family and for the many close friends I had made in Connecticut. We didn't have six bathrooms and the mailman didn't bring the mail in his Cadillac, but somehow we managed to eke out a fair measure of happiness (she says sardonically). Maybe it depends where one's values lie.

I feel it only fair to mention here I have read some fine articles about our boys that have stuck to the facts and still managed to come up with compelling stories. Doug Smith wrote two pieces for *USA Today* that recognized their potential. The first, "Double Promise," appeared in 1998, when Thomas and James both played for Harvard, and speculates both might be pro material. A further article by Doug in April 1999 suggests James, having become the top-ranked college player, might be ready to take a break from Harvard and join his brother on the pro circuit.

In the August 18 2002 *New York Times*, Selena Roberts wrote a lovely piece on how James handled scoliosis and his advice to others with the affliction. In this piece she actually reported exactly what I said to her—quite a rarity. A lengthy article by Richard Osborn for the May 2002 issue of *Inside Tennis* sees James as "the intersection of

Mix It Up, Make It Nice

125th Street and Harvard Yard," pointing out how comfortable he feels in each venue. I learned a few things I didn't know about my youngest son from a feature in *The New York Times Magazine* of August 28 2005, written by Howard Axelrod. Until I read that, I had no idea of the tremendous pain he suffered from shingles after his father's death. I suppose he felt I had enough to contend with at the time. I particularly enjoyed a thoughtful piece by William Rhoden in the September 6 2005 *New York Times* in which he compares James to Arthur Ashe, and questions whether James can accomplish what he voiced as a teenager playing in his first US Open—"to have a character as great as him is an even harder accomplishment." Christopher Clarey, also in *The New York Times*, wrote about James's "climb out of a painful place," and I enjoyed George Vecsey's article from the same paper in September 2005 in which he talks about James's rowdy supporters, particularly his brother Thomas.

Lisa Olson wrote at least three pieces about James for the New York *Daily News*, each one outstanding. The first, entitled "New Brains, Please" describes her take on the Hewitt/Blake controversy at the 2001 US Open, when Lleyton made some remarks most listeners agreed were racist. In another article, when the two met again the following year, she wonders at the way James's demeanor seemed to rub off on Hewitt, normally a much more fiery player given to fist-pumps and frequent shouts of "C'mon." After James's unexpected defeat of Rafael Nadal at the 2005 US Open she wrote a particularly exuberant piece about his amazing comeback. I love her humor, and I would like to thank her personally for all the praise she heaps on James. Finally, I'm grateful for several articles Mike Daly wrote about James for the *Connecticut Post*. Mike and I often walk our dogs together and James went to school with Mike's son, so whenever James is in town he will find time to have lunch with Mike, which always generates another article.

Up to now our boys had seen little serious competition. We decided it was time for them to find out what kind of tennis talent New England had to offer.

... to travel hopefully is a better thing than to arrive, and the true success is to labour.

—ROBERT LOUIS STEVENSON

Chapter 5:
A Tennis Education

OUR FIRST REAL EXPERIENCE with tournaments in New England came when Thomas was in the 14s and James in the 12s. Before that, they had played a few tournaments in New York, but nothing we took seriously, probably because of the results. We have a picture of a very young Thomas holding a trophy but I don't recall which tournament he won. He may have played in a few 12-and-under tournaments, but with little success. James acquired his first trophy when he entered an 8-and-under tournament and no one else showed up.

When they began to play in New England, they first had to enter what were then called "B" tournaments—later called "Challenger" level. They eventually played in "A" tournaments or "Championship" level, which made them eligible for a New England ranking. (The whole format is different now.)

We soon discovered our sons possessed unfortunate birth dates—December 28 (James) and December 29 (Thomas). When they were born, tennis was not uppermost in our minds, and Tom, happy with the huge tax break he received the year Thomas arrived, urged me to try to duplicate it with James. Ironically, my due date for both had been in January, which would have put them in a different age bracket when they started playing tournaments and given them a huge advantage.

When they began to take junior tennis seriously, both wished they had not been in such a hurry to come into the world. The tournament year ended on December 31, so in any age group they often had to compete with players one and sometimes almost two years older. They complained so much about the injustice of it I almost felt guilty for having them early. I found out later the cutoff date, which had been October 1 when my son Chris played junior tournaments (his birthday is September 20—he was also three weeks early), had changed the year before Thomas and James began to compete. I seem to specialize in bad tennis birthdays as well as a propensity for early labor. To make matters even worse, the USTA saw fit to change the December 31 date after James's final junior year. It almost seemed like a vendetta. Yet on looking back, I may have unwittingly done them a good turn because they both had to work harder to compete with the stronger players in their respective groups. At the time they didn't appreciate that. To juniors, it's all about winning.

As James matured, competing first in college and then on the tour, he would often say he wished he hadn't taken his junior losses so seriously. With the emphasis on winning, especially in the earlier years, young players often ignore bad habits that should be corrected before they become too ingrained. Brian, who always looks at the larger picture, changed James's forehand when he was still in the 12s. James predictably lost a few matches because of this, prompting him to ask Brian if he felt bad

A Tennis Education

he had "ruined his career." We all laughed at this, mainly at the idea this little pipsqueak might think he had a shot at a career in tennis. As James grew older, he admitted it was one of the best things Brian did for him, and given the current recognition of James's forehand as one of the best in tennis, time bore him out. As always, Brian knew best.

Brian advocates moderation in everything—praise but not exultation for a win and helpful advice and suggestions after a loss. Parents who become too effusive over a victory often place undue and completely unproductive pressure on their children. I have heard some parents, upset over a loss, actually become abusive to their child. I find this hard to believe. The child feels bad enough about losing without added censure from those who should be providing encouragement and support. Watching James play in one of his earlier tournaments, Tom praised him, saying he didn't mind he lost because he was doing the right things. Unfortunately, James did mind. It's difficult to get that point across to a youngster, especially one who has just lost a match he felt he should have won.

I recall watching a 12-year-old who regularly won every match he played, but his forehand didn't look quite right, even to my largely untrained eye. I mentioned this to his father and suggested now would be the best time to change it.

"But he wins all his matches. Why should we change anything?" he asked me, possibly seeing my suggestion as a motive to make life easier for James.

I didn't pursue it, but by the time that boy played in 16 and 18 competition, he had ceased to win all his matches, and eventually stopped playing altogether.

Another time, when James played in zonal competition in the 12-and-under age group, we watched him lose every match he played. Becoming more upset with each loss he threw a major tantrum after his last match. One perceptive coach took him aside and assured him he had more talent than any of the other players. James didn't want to hear that—he just wanted to win—now, not some vague time in the future.

The group Thomas had to compete in was especially strong. Four players stayed at the top of that group and seemed unshakeable. In the 14s he always seemed to draw one of the top seeds, and would lose badly in the first round. I recall one of the first New England tournaments he entered. We pulled into the parking lot next to an impressive-looking car with a license plate reading MIRSKY. Checking the draw, we saw that name again—Adam Mirsky, the top seed, and Thomas had to play him in the first round. We were soon pulling out of that parking lot.

Another time I entered Thomas in a tournament in Cape Cod, mainly so my friend Joyce and I could spend a weekend at one of our favorite places. Joyce and I worked together in the Dean's office at Sacred Heart University. We discovered we thought alike on many issues, great and small, so we enjoyed spending more time with each other than those hours at the office.

Again, Thomas drew the top seed, Josh Hausman, and lost gracefully; 6-0, 6-0. Ironically, Thomas and Josh later became teammates and very good friends on the Harvard team. By then Thomas had blossomed and earned the number-one singles spot in his sophomore year. They were, and still are, such good friends that if they had to play each other in a tournament neither seemed happy about it. Thomas wanted to win, but didn't want to beat Josh. When in his second year in the 16-and-under age bracket Thomas did manage to beat one of those elite players, I wasn't prepared for it. I regularly booked a motel for one night. The first time he made it into the final day of a tournament, I had to scurry around to find accommodation for a second night.

Our education about tournaments and what they might lead to began in 1991 when Thomas received his first invitation to the prestigious Wightman tournament in Massachusetts. I recall Thomas's quite uncharacteristic reaction to his invitation. Reading from the letter, he gleefully informed us, as one of the top players in New

A Tennis Education

England, he had been chosen to take part in this tournament. He didn't know what this meant and neither did we. Later we discovered it is an annual tournament that helps to determine which players from New England will qualify for various USTA national tournaments. Thomas didn't do well in the tournament that year, and the following year, his first year in the 16s, he didn't qualify. Not happy with this, he had me call the authorities to find out if there was a mistake. (There wasn't.) This perceived slight might have had something to do with his unexpectedly winning the Wightman tournament for two consecutive years in 1994 and 1995.

Sam Josephs, Evan Paushter, James, John Portlock at Wightman in Massachusetts

That year turned out to be the only year we didn't go to Wightman. From 1993 to 1998 (James's last year as a junior), our yearly trek to the tournament became a ritual to which we all looked forward. Thomas and James had become friends with most of the other players and they all enjoyed spending the week together. Naturally, Tom and I came to know their parents, so we enjoyed it too. The site for the tournament was a private tennis club laid out in beautiful grounds with all the amenities you associate with a private club. I recall Ernie Paushter (James's best friend's father) relaxing on his chaise under a Wightman tree, smiling contentedly and saying, "I just want my son to keep playing well enough to get me to places like this."

We had also become friends with the Dalys who lived in Wellesley not far from Wightman. Matt Daly, their youngest son, was in James's age group. For most of their junior years, the other New England players were in awe of Matt. He had won the 14s National tournament in San Antonio, and possessed an Easter Bowl trophy—two tournaments in which New England players rarely acquit themselves well. Even more impressive to James was the fact Reebok gave him free clothing.

Ben and Joan Daly own a large house; they graciously provided accommodation for us and several other players from Connecticut for the duration of the tournament. That was another reason we so looked forward to Wightman. The camaraderie between the boys and the parents during that week turned into something special, which we often remember fondly. We have remained friends to this day, and those players (and some of the parents) now make up part of the J-Block—James's exclusive cheering section, which originated in 2005 at the Pilot Pen tournament in New Haven. The rest of the J-Block is made up of James's many non-tennis playing friends, mostly from high school and college.

Besides the Wightman tournament, which was mandatory for entry into national competition, there were many other lesser tournaments throughout the year. To improve your ranking, you would play in as many of these as possible, hoping to beat a player who was ranked higher than you. Those players aspiring to national status (and who wasn't?) also had to compete in at least two of the four NNQ (New England Qualifier) tournaments.

One year when James had improved enough that he had a good chance of playing on a national level, he blithely skipped the first two NNQs. Brian and I both worried something might happen to keep him out of the two that remained. I don't recall what kept him out of the first, but he chose to go on a skiing trip instead of playing the second. Looking back, I wonder how he managed to get us to agree to this. Surprisingly, Tom had no problem with it, but Brian and I had visions of broken bones (James was new to skiing and extremely reckless) and we heaved a huge sigh of relief when he came back intact.

A player in New England must compete with the best in five states—Maine, New Hampshire, Massachusetts, Rhode Island and Connecticut. The USTA-determined quota of players for our section of the country always seemed unfairly small. When our boys were competing, they typically invited only the top four players in the section, with the fifth player having a chance of getting in if he were ranked high enough. I can't recall many of their earlier matches—probably because of the mediocre results—so I will rely on the New England Yearbooks I still have. I believe they both played in a few 10-and-under tournaments (Thomas would have played these in the Eastern rather than the New England section) and someone told me James had received an "honorable mention" one year, but I can't recall which year and that book is missing.

Thomas appears for the first time in the 1991 book as the 11th best player in the 14-and-under category, not high enough for national competition. James would have been in his first year of 12-and-under but his name is nowhere to be found, not even an "honorable mention" after the 36 best players. But I do remember he began to show some promise in his second year in that age group, and the 1992 yearbook bears me out, for he is listed among the top 10 players in New England. They would list the younger players alphabetically, hoping this would discourage the kind of cutthroat competition that often takes place in junior tennis. It didn't work. All the 12-year-olds knew exactly which position each player held on the list, and I thought the competition here was just as fierce, if not fiercer than with older players. Thomas, now in his first year in the 16-and-under category, achieved number 20 on the list that year, still far from national qualification.

Mix It Up, Make It Nice

While many of these early tournaments have faded into obscurity, I vividly recall James, aged 11, competing in one of his first tournaments in Canton Connecticut. It began with him almost being denied entry. He had been excluded from a previous tournament (his ranking wasn't high enough), but with the assurance he would have an automatic entry into the next one. When I called for his start time and found he was not in the draw, he became highly indignant, so I took it up with the authorities and got him in. The tournament director was not happy I went over his head and his attitude toward us proved it. Traffic was bad and we arrived about 10 minutes late for the first match, incurring a three-game penalty. At the time the format for 12 and under competition was one set (first to get six games) against each player in your flight, so three games down looked insurmountable. I'm sure the director went by the rules, but the penalty seemed harsh. Luckily, James drew a first-year player who was even smaller than he and managed to make up the deficit and win the match.

Subsequent matches proved much more difficult, one of them against the best player in New England (so the other parents told me—at the time I didn't know the pecking order). I particularly remember watching this match because James was trading shot for shot with his opponent and I began to think maybe he could pull off a win. Then on a crucial point he missed an easy overhead. I over-reacted, burying my face in my hands, and James looked up at just that moment. Brian, who also coaches parents (on their behavior), told me this is a definite no-no. If your child misses a shot he feels bad enough about it without added censure from onlookers. Today, other parents often ask me how I stay so calm at matches. That experience in the 12s may have a lot to do with it.

Despite the missed overhead, James managed to eke out a victory, won the other matches in his flight and found himself in the finals. Now he had to play another well-known New England player, Dean Chiungos, who had won all his matches without losing a game. They played the regular best two out of three sets and James achieved an unexpected upset win. This may have been the first

72

A Tennis Education

time anyone in tennis circles had heard of James Blake. The tournament director must have had pressing business elsewhere, for he wasn't there to present James with his trophy.

About this time, at one of his annual check-ups, the doctor noticed a pronounced curve in James's back and recommended seeing an orthopedic doctor. The first one we went to diagnosed it as scoliosis and talked about doing surgery and putting a steel rod in his back. This seemed a little drastic so we went home to think about it. Next, we took James to our chiropractor. He told us he could do nothing to help James, but he would recommend his case to the Shriners Hospital for Crippled Children in Springfield Massachusetts. This could be a way to avoid surgery. He also said if accepted the treatment would be without cost. Naturally, we jumped at it.

The first time I took James to Springfield we had to spend almost the entire day there. They examined James, ascertained the extent of the curve, then told us to come back later to try on his brace. After lunch at Friendly's we returned to the hospital. When we left several hours later, a hard plastic brace encased James's body from his armpits to the top of his thighs. He sat awkwardly in the passenger seat, and I kept glancing over at him to see how he was handling this. They told him he would have to wear the brace 18 hours each day until he stopped growing—all of his high school years, and possibly longer. When I asked him how he felt about this, he surprised me by his stoicism.

Some of the heartbreaking cases we had seen during our long stay at the hospital made him realize he should consider himself one of the lucky ones. We saw children with missing limbs, and others whose deformities were much worse than James's. He even credits the experience with helping him become less bratty on the tennis court, by realizing how lucky he was just to be there. He did, however, become sensitive about the brace when he started high school, something I only discovered much later when he discussed the experience with reporters. During the teen years no one wants to be different and he now admits this affected him socially. Although he hadn't finished growing at age 17 when he entered Harvard, he adamantly refused to wear the brace any longer. He didn't intend to jeopardize his college life.

James grew considerably during his junior year in high school, necessitating a bigger brace. We made the hour-and-a-half trek to Springfield several times during that year, coming back each time with a new brace, all at no cost to us.

"Going to Shriners was such a positive experience for me," James said. "It made me appreciate at a young age that I had a lot to be thankful for." Today, he gives back to the Shriners by contributing to them as one of his favorite charities, and by visiting the young patients at the hospital in Tampa whenever he can squeeze it into his busy schedule.

Wearing the brace for all those years kept the curve from getting worse, but James still has a pronounced bend in his spine which is all too visible when he changes his shirt on the court. We and his doctors have often marveled he can play as well as he does with this handicap.

Despite the scoliosis, James's future had begun to look bright, but it dimmed considerably when he moved into the 14-and-under age bracket. By now most of his contemporaries (especially those in their second year) had begun their growth spurt. Not just taller than James, they had also started to bulk up, and many of them developed impressive muscles in their legs and arms. This proved another source of frustration for James. He thought he would never grow. Thomas had grown early and already stood 6'4", and with two half-brothers both 6'5", James felt like the midget in the family. Finally in his junior year in high school he started to shoot up as well as bulk up, but before that he suffered a lot of frustration. Boys in his own age group, those with whom he could compete a year earlier, would regularly beat him badly.

Once again what seemed misfortune for James may have set the stage for his later success, and once again he

A Tennis Education

benefited from having his brother blaze the trail on the tournament circuit. "I wasn't very good until the 18s," said Thomas. "I lost a lot in the 14s and 16s." When Thomas did start winning, James was still in the 14s, and seeing his brother start to blossom inspired him to greater efforts. Because of his size he had to work much harder to achieve any kind of results, and I believe this led him to develop a strong work ethic, which became even stronger when he began to have some success. However it wasn't until his second year in the 16s and both years in the 18s he achieved successes that surprised his family, his coach and quite a few others, notably boys (and their parents) who had perceived no threat when scheduled to play James Blake.

By dint of this hard work ethic, James worked his way up to the number-three position in New England in his second year in the 14 and under age group. This meant he qualified for national competition—something new to us. Tom took him to two national events in the summer where he lost quickly, so we hardly noticed they were gone. I took him to the National Indoors in Chicago that year—more on this later.

Although he really began to shine in the 18s, Thomas did grind out a few good results in his second year in the 16 and under age group. In one NNQ tournament he had to play the top seed for a place in the final five. I settled down to watch, thinking it would soon be over, hoping only that Thomas would make the score respectable. He ended up losing in a third-set tiebreak after holding a match point. This meant he had to play the next day to determine the positions of the final five players. I thought he would be in no shape to play after this huge disappointment; also during the night he developed a fever and couldn't face breakfast (a sure indication he was sick). He insisted on playing and somehow managed to win his match. I think he felt so ill he just went for shots with careless abandon and luckily most of them fell in. This tournament went a long way towards making him eligible for his first invitation to national tournaments.

Mix It Up, Make It Nice

By now Thomas and James considered tennis their major sport, but they still enjoyed other sports. They played for local Little League baseball teams, and both were selected to play on their respective All-Star teams. When we moved to Connecticut they tried their hands at skiing, which many of their new friends enjoyed. James signed up for indoor track and spent one year on the high school wrestling team. They asked him because he was so small for his age and they needed someone in a certain weight category. This came at a time when he was beginning to take tennis more seriously, and I wondered about missing so much practice time. He assured me playing twice a week would be enough, and claimed the conditioning he went through for wrestling would help his tennis. He was right—conditioning plays a much larger role in tennis than most junior players realize.

At the annual wrestling awards ceremony they gave James the "light bulb" award for spending the most time on the mat looking up at the lights. That proved the end of his wrestling career.

They had other interests besides sports. Before we introduced them to tennis, we instilled in them a love of reading. They saw we always carried a book with us and they adopted the same habit. School always took precedence over tennis or any other sport. If a conflict arose between tennis and school, school always won. We actually turned down invitations to several important tournaments because it would have taken them out of school.

Thomas learned to play the bass baritone and became a valuable member of the high school band. He also participated in Math meets as a member of an organization called the JETS. In his grade school days, James became a proficient juggler. I took time out from work one day to watch him perform. I held my breath as he climbed up and down a stepladder while keeping five balls in the air. Trying again to follow his brother's lead, James flirted briefly with two different band instruments, one of them the sousaphone, which seemed bigger than him. I wasn't sorry when that venture ended.

A Tennis Education

James loved baseball almost as much as tennis and was fortunate to be on a good team, Blue Sky Bar. His coach, Joe Gasparino, realizing James's value to the team wanted him at every practice and every game. I told him if James had a tennis tournament, that took priority. Luckily, there weren't many conflicts. Whenever I run into his coach today, he claims credit for James's career because he allowed him time off from baseball to play tennis. Even with the time off, James helped his team to a championship.

Although James had already played tennis on a national level when he started high school, he was still eager to play for the Fairfield Mustangs. His brother, now a senior and playing in national tournaments too, opted to stay on the team. Some of their new friends on the national circuit expressed their surprise. New to the national experience, our sons didn't know the unwritten rules—the vast majority of players who are good enough for national competition consider high school tennis beneath them. Our boys liked the team aspect, winning for the team, cheering for their friends. This continued at Harvard and in James's case with Davis Cup. They love the camaraderie that goes with team play.

James, though still small for his age, earned the number-two spot behind his brother at number one. In his freshman year he encountered some strong opposition, often from boys three or four years older, but he also bruised the egos of some older players who judged James only by his size. In his four years in high school he acquired an 80-3 record and went through his last two years without surrendering a set. One local reporter said James playing high school tennis was like pitting a Sherman tank against a popgun.

I vividly recall one of those three losses. Playing in New Canaan, James lost a close match, which turned out to be the decider. Thomas had won his match so James felt he had let his team down. I remember how upset he was, but what I remember most is how understanding and consoling Thomas was towards his brother. They both felt the hurt of losing a close match, but Thomas seemed more concerned with comforting his brother—such a welcome change from how they used to fight just a few years earlier.

Some of the smaller high schools presented little challenge, so always competitive, our boys devised a way to lend interest. Playing on adjacent courts, they would try to be the first to claim victory. At one match both had a match point at the same time. James, acutely aware of the situation, kept casting glances over toward the next court. Probably recalling all the times Thomas beat him while growing up, he hurriedly smashed an overhead to win the last point. "I won," he exulted, throwing up his arms in victory, to the amazement of his opponent who had barely won a point much less a game. Thomas ended his match and cast a reproving look at his brother, as he graciously shook hands with his opponent at the net. Realizing the situation, James had the grace to look sheepish as he shook hands, but he still basked in the glow of a rare victory over his brother.

In those days there were rules about the number of high school matches you could play if you were in a tournament at the end of that week, so they tried to schedule tournaments so they could help the team most. Even so, the Mustangs never won a team championship during the five years Thomas and James played. That proved a big disappointment, for both valued team success over individual glory. Recently I found one of James's recommendation letters for college. James had told the writer he had won his high school match that day but the team had lost—he would have preferred the other way 'round. That team spirit impressed her.

What I remember most about New England junior tournaments is Tom and I often spent our weekends traveling in different directions all over New England. If they lost early, we salvaged Sundays, but both improving on this level and it was sometimes Monday morning before we compared notes.

"What happened to our weekend?" I would ask on a Monday morning, as another workweek loomed.

A Tennis Education

"You tell me," Tom would say in that annoying way he had of throwing a question back at you.

We often sacrificed our weekends to tennis, but as Tom pointed out to one interviewer, "We've made sacrifices, but these are sacrifices of love because the kids wanted it, and we were willing to do it."

Although Tom sometimes seemed a stern disciplinarian, he loved his sons so much he made much larger sacrifices whenever he felt it would help them and improve their characters. If either one showed an interest in a certain area, Tom would spare no expense on the books he would buy on that subject. Before Thomas could read, he was obsessed by dinosaurs. We still have some of the beautiful illustrated books his father bought for him. When James had to write an assignment on sharks, Tom added several books on that subject to their library.

Spending time with and helping our sons seemed no sacrifice to us. We enjoyed the time spent together. I don't believe there's a children's museum in the area we haven't visited at least once, and we often spent entire Saturday mornings at the library helping them with their choice of books. After the Armory became a homeless shelter and we adults couldn't play there, we still drove down on weekends. We both volunteered as coaches so the boys could take advantage of the free clinics.

Ivy League schools don't offer athletic scholarships, so sending them to Harvard when they had many offers of full scholarships to prestigious universities presented a huge financial burden. Our sacrifices have borne more fruit than we could ever have imagined. If Tom can see our sons now, he must realize how those sacrifices have paid off.

In 1993, the first year Thomas qualified for the National Hard Court tournament, we began to give up more than our weekends to tennis. Now we said goodbye to idyllic summer vacations in Cape Cod. It turned out to be the first of six consecutive years we spent our summer vacation in early August in Kalamazoo Michigan.

Mix It Up, Make It Nice

*Start by doing what's necessary; then do what's possible;
and suddenly you are doing the impossible.*

—ST. FRANCIS OF ASSISI

Chapter 6:
Nationals

MENTION "KALAMAZOO" TO any somewhat serious young tennis player and he will immediately know what it signifies. Kalamazoo Michigan has become Mecca for the aspiring male tennis player. We still have a button proclaiming "Yes, there really is a Kalamazoo," acquired on our first trip there. For many years after we first heard of it and what it meant, it had seemed to us like a mythical, faraway kingdom, which you could only reach on a magic carpet.

This unassuming town in the heart of the country is the site, each year in August, of the boys 16 and 18 National Hard Court Championships. Now in its 65th year, such great names as Rod Laver, Andre Agassi, Stan

Mix It Up, Make It Nice

Smith, John McEnroe, Michael Chang, Pete Sampras and Jim Courier have played as juniors on its courts. Amazingly, reading down the list of winners in the Kalamazoo handbook, you find few of these illustrious names. Laver did win both singles and doubles in 1956, while in 1987 Courier and Chang battled for the title, with Chang emerging as the winner. McEnroe and Agassi both won doubles trophies, but never made it through the singles competition. Andy Roddick and James both lost in their final match.

We made our first trip there in 1992, Thomas's second year in 16-and-under competition. When it seemed he might have a chance to play at Kalamazoo, we did all we could to make it happen. At the time the quota for New England stood at four, and we knew Thomas was fifth on the list. I called a friend at USTA who suggested he play some out-of-section tournaments to enhance his chances of getting in as an alternate. It must have worked. I recall how excited we all were when we heard he had been selected.

As we drove into Kalamazoo we saw huge billboards announcing the tournament. We couldn't believe it. We felt as if we had hit the big time. Thomas registered, picked up his goodie bag filled with samples from the host of sponsors, and then we checked the draw. It consisted of 128 players from all over the United States. In the upper right-hand corner was the list of seeded players—32 of the best young players in the country. We stood in awe. We had been so happy for Thomas just to get into the draw. How good must those seeded players be? If someone had told us that five years hence we would see our youngest son's name listed in the number-two spot on that right-hand corner, we would have questioned his sanity.

Thomas played his first match on August 8—my birthday—and he gave me the best gift possible—he won a hard-fought match. For his next match he had to play one of the seeded players, Marcus Fluitt. He took the match to three sets, and had his chances to win it, but nerves kicked in on the crucial points and he couldn't pull off the upset.

Nationals

After a player loses in the main draw, he goes into the "back" or "feed-in" draw. He then plays another player who has lost. This guarantees each competitor will play at least two matches. As more and better players lose, play becomes highly competitive, and the winner of the back draw enjoys almost as much prestige as the main winner, with an entire page devoted to photos of those players in the following year's program. Thomas lost his back draw match, and we headed home, stopping on the way to visit my brother and his family who live in Adrian Michigan.

Thomas qualified for the tournament for the next two years, but never won another match there. In his first year in the 18s he injured his back and had to withdraw. In July of his second year in that age category he surprised us all by getting to the finals of the National Clay Court Championships in Louisville Kentucky, for clay was by no means his favorite surface. His next tournament was on the hard courts in Kalamazoo. Since his style of play lent itself more to quicker surfaces, we thought, with his confidence riding high, he would do well in his last appearance there. Unfortunately, even though he ate Cap'n Crunch for breakfast before his match as he had every day in Louisville, he lost his first match in the main draw as well as his consolation match in the back draw. So much for superstition.

Thomas also played for two consecutive years in the International Grass Court Championships in Philadelphia, where he acquitted himself well. Ironically, playing in the semifinals there in his second year, he won the match against Marcus Fluitt. Marcus had beaten Thomas in his first loss in national competition, and Thomas ended his junior years with a victory over the same player. It turned out to be Thomas's last junior win. He finished his junior career as the 18th-best player in the country. No one in the family expected James to top this. That year, James held the 159th position on the national list.

New England players, probably because they have to play indoors for a good part of the year, have a reputation for doing poorly in national outdoor tournaments. The big names all come from such states as Florida, California

Mix It Up, Make It Nice

and Georgia—states where you can play outdoors all year 'round. When James first qualified for national play, he upheld the New England tradition. I don't recall he won any matches in the 14s nationals. He began to play better in the 16s and we thought they would both be invited to Kalamazoo in 1995—Thomas's last year as a junior player and James's first year in a new age group. New England's quota that year was four and although James was in fifth place, the boy just ahead of him had told him he was spending his summer in Africa, so James counted on making it. I can still hear the frustration in his voice when he opened the letter expecting to see his name on the list. "Reeve told me he wasn't going," he said in disbelief. I appealed to the USTA, but that year they only took the four top players from the section, no alternates.

Now we had a dilemma on our hands. James had to decide whether to go with us to Kalamazoo or stay with one of his friends while we went with Thomas. It was a tough decision because he would have to watch players who had made it into the draw from weaker sections, and who he felt he could have beaten. I still have the piece of paper on which he listed the pros and cons while he tried to make up his mind. In the con list he has "get mad when I see people I can beat." In the pro section he lists "visit Uncle Albert" and "play golf with Dad." I like to think those weighed heavily in his decision to go with us.

We developed a pattern during those six consecutive summers of driving to Kalamazoo. We would leave Fairfield as early as possible so we could reach my brother's house (Uncle Albert's) in Adrian Michigan, just over the Ohio border, by about 7:00 p.m. Al and his wife Mandy would save dinner for us. These dinners were something we all looked forward to. Al and Mandy grew all their own vegetables, baked their own bread and both are terrific cooks. One of our favorites is their spinach pie, even though we're not great fans of that particular vegetable. Albert told me it was easy to make and wrote out the recipe for me—it covers two 8½ by 11 pages. You start by making the phyllo dough, which has to be rolled out, folded and rolled out several more times. I attempted it once and it turned out well, but it took ages for me to clean up the kitchen, which seemed to be totally blanketed in flour. I never tried it again.

We would stay the night in Adrian and then drive the three or four more hours to Kalamazoo the next day. Then, depending on the tennis results, we would spend time with Al and Mandy on the way home. Until our last year there, we had plenty of time for visiting before heading home.

Thomas had become a force in New England tennis and held the number-three ranking in his first and second years in the 18-and-under category. This meant he qualified for all the national tournaments. In his first year in this category he and I went by ourselves because James (second year in the 14s and also number-three in New England) qualified for the boys hard court nationals in San Antonio Texas, so Tom went with him. That turned out to be a bad year. Our boys lost their first matches in both the main and back draws.

In November James qualified for the National Indoors in Chicago, held during Thanksgiving break. Thomas, still 16 but forced to play 18-and-under tournaments because of his late birthday, qualified for the National Indoors, held in Texas at the same time. Off we went in different directions again. Tom flew with Thomas to Texas while James and I drove to Chicago. Driving through Philadelphia a policeman pulled me over for speeding (my children find that hard to believe). Politely, I appealed to the officer that I was traveling much slower than the huge trucks hurtling by us, and he agreed. James, still small and sporting braids, his latest hair experiment, nestled cozily in his heated passenger seat, swathed in a blanket, a pillow behind his head. The officer looked at his sweet, innocent face and said, "Okay, lady. But make sure your daughter has her seat belt on." Stifling a smile, I assured him I would.

We made it to Chicago without further mishap. James won his first match and everything looked rosy. Brian Gottfried, a former top-10 player, happened to watch that match and seemed interested in James. "Who's the kid with the dreads?" he inquired of those near him. "They're not dreads, they're braids," I enlightened him. "And he's James Blake." I didn't ask him why he showed interest. Maybe he recognized potential even at that early age.

After that, disaster struck. James drew Christopher Ma, one of the seeds, in the next round. Playing well, he went three sets and had a match point, but nerves got the better of him and he couldn't pull off the win. After that match, he was inconsolable. Zombie-like, he sat in the lounge staring into space. I tried to talk to him. He didn't want to listen. I asked him to come and eat. He wasn't hungry. I didn't know what to do. He only snapped out of it when it came time for him to play in the back draw. Judging from the warm-up, it seemed James would have little trouble with this opponent. I anticipated a win and hoped it would make him feel better. Unfortunately, it didn't happen. James played badly and lost again.

Here's where my brother (God bless him) saved the day. We checked out of our motel and drove the short distance to Adrian Michigan. The ride seemed interminable, with James still brooding about his losses. It did no good to tell him he should treat this as a learning experience, or losing a tennis match is not the end of the world. To him, it did seem like the end of his world.

My brother's house, as usual, overflowed with people. Several of his seven children, with various friends, were visiting for Thanksgiving. Though quite a bit older than James, they included him in their games and discovered he had a talent for a game called "Taboo" where you have to get your partner to say a word without the help of several banned words. The ego boost helped to make him forget the past few days, and the long ride back to Fairfield was much more pleasant.

In spite of his losses, he somehow acquired a national ranking that year—#88 on the list. I sometimes wonder if the 87 boys ranked ahead of him are still playing tennis. I recognize most of the names, a few of whom turned professional, but certainly none have become household names. The preceding year he was way down at the bottom of the list, at 159, and one USTA official told me he was lucky to be on it. In those days no one, least of all

James, would have picked him to rise to the heights he enjoys today.

Just like Thomas, when James moved into the 16-and-under group he was still 14, turning 15 three days before the end of the year. He still hadn't grown appreciably, but played well enough to qualify for the National Indoor tournament in his first year. This turned into another bad experience, similar to the Chicago fiasco.

The 16s Indoors takes place in Massachusetts—very convenient for us. It fell on me to take him to this one. He won his first round, and then came up against one of the top seeds, Ryan Sachire. Although his opponent was much bigger and stronger, James played well and had his chances to win the match. Again it didn't happen and he lost a close match—6-4 in the third set. In the back draw he played another tall, strong boy who happened to have his hair styled in Mohawk fashion. James lost again. Still fuming when we got in the car to go home, he started casting around for something, anything, to destroy, luckily finding only a ballpoint pen. As he took out his rage on the pen, he said "I lost to a guy with a Mohawk." Ironic, considering the variety of hairstyles he has sported since then.

The first time James played at Kalamazoo, his second year in the 16s, he upheld the New England tradition, lost quickly in both the main and back draws, and we were soon on our way back to Adrian to spend time with the relatives.

Later that year, however, he did begin to attract some attention on the national level. In his second year at the Indoors in Massachusetts, he went on a run all the way to the finals. The first seeded player he beat was a tall boy who seemed used to winning. In fact his mother became quite vocal about how poorly her son had played in losing to James. She had a difficult time accepting a diminutive, unseeded and largely unknown player had scored a victory over her son. James proved it was no fluke by winning his way into the finals. Since the tournament was close to home, quite a few of James's friends came up to watch him play in his first National final.

Perhaps James was overwhelmed by having come so far when no one expected it, and it showed in his game. I could tell from the warm-up things would not go well, and he proved me right. His play in this match bore little resemblance to the way he had played to get this far, and he lost badly to David Martin, a very good first-year player. In the photos we have of the trophy presentation, James's face reflects how unhappy he felt. He may not have been able to win, but he knew he could have played a better match.

James's first junior national final in Massachusetts.
You can tell by his face he lost to David Martin.

Brian, always upbeat, assured him it was because this was his first time in the finals of a big tournament. "The next time this happens," he said, "you'll play much better." Of course he was right as usual, but it was a whole year before James found himself in that position again.

Now in his first year in the 18-and-under group, he was playing well enough to be invited to all the national tournaments. He had some success at the Clay Courts in Kentucky. Tom went with him to that one, but I remember

Nationals

James calling me to tell me he had a win over a player who was ranked well ahead of him. Because he had begun to step up his game, we expected him to fare much better at Kalamazoo this year. We set off with high expectations, only to have them dashed when we saw the draw. James had drawn Kevin Kim, the top seed, in the first round. So again he upheld the New England tradition and lost badly in the first round, 6-1, 6-1. He did, however, win two or three matches in the back draw, which was an improvement over the previous Blake performances. Kevin went on to win the tournament that year, and soon after turned pro. He and James have played each other several times on the professional tour, and James has managed to avenge that junior loss.

In the French Open in 2005, Cliff Drysdale, the announcer, observed James and Kevin Kim were the last two American hopes left in the draw, and his comments implied James would be the best bet to stay in the draw. A few years can make a huge difference. The announcers like to add a little color with stories from the players' pasts. I think Cliff would have liked the story of how badly James lost to Kevin when they played on the junior circuit.

Just as I showed little confidence when I only booked a motel room for one night for their New England tournaments, I showed the same lack of confidence for national matches. When we drove to a tournament, it didn't matter because we left whenever they lost, but if we had to fly it became tricky. When do you book the return flight? You don't want to book it for the last day—that would certainly jinx them.

In November of that year Tom took James to Texas for the National Indoor Tournament. I stayed in Fairfield with Thomas, who had come home from Harvard for Thanksgiving. I thought I showed more confidence than usual when I booked return airline tickets for Saturday. That would put James into the semifinals. It turned out to be his first National title. The tournament officials decreed the finals should be best three out of five sets. James played well against his friend Robert Kendrick, and won it in five (proving Brian's prediction).

He and his father had to come back from Texas on standby, finally arriving home in the wee hours. I still recall James's comment to me that morning at about 4. "Nice confidence, Mom." He was smiling though, because besides winning the tournament, they had given him the Sportsmanship Award—something in his racket-throwing days we all predicted would never happen. In fact, he told me about this award before he mentioned he had won the tournament.

After breaking the ice with this tournament, James's confidence soared. In this last year of junior tournaments, no one in New England could beat him. His next national tournament was the Clay Courts in Louisville, Kentucky, where three years earlier his brother had been runner-up in both singles and doubles. For the first time James saw his name in the column of seeds. Although not in the top eight, he was happy to be listed with the nine through 16 seeds. After winning two rounds he had to play another seed—David Martin, the player who had beaten him in his first National final. Normally, we try not to look ahead in the draw, taking each match as it comes, but I know James wanted the chance to play David again. It turned out to be a nail-biter but James prevailed in three sets. When he plays against someone who has a victory over him, it gives him added incentive to win. In the semifinals he played Andrew Park, a player known for returning virtually every ball that made it over the net. James had to fight for every point but he won a hard-fought match.

In the final match James had to play the top seed, Rudy Rake. Rudy had breezed through to this point. James had never played him but when Rudy first came on the scene I recall the New England players looking at him with awe. After watching him play a first-round match in the 16s, James commented, "This is a national tournament, and he played like it was a high school match." It seemed no one could come close to beating him. Rudy was the heavy favorite to win, and everyone thought James would settle for runner-up as his brother did three years earlier, but James played the match of his life and chalked up his second national title. We enjoyed a pleasant ride home from Louisville—a huge contrast to some of our rides home when James had lost matches he felt he should have won.

That Indoor Nationals in November was the beginning of a string of 49 victories for James, which didn't end until August of the following year. He won every match he played in New England as well as his second National title at the Clay Courts in Kentucky, then won his way to the finals at Kalamazoo that year, finally losing to Rudy to end the string. During that spell he also won all of his high school matches, as well as the State championship, which didn't figure in the total.

At this point in James's tennis life, the USTA began to notice him. We received a telephone call just before the hard court nationals offering some money to defray expenses. When both boys were playing nationals, going in different directions, we had appealed to the USTA for help but apparently their rankings weren't high enough. Now they offered us $500. Ever the persuasive salesman, Tom seized the opportunity to make them double the amount, so for the first time we felt justified in staying at the tournament hotel. In previous years we had stayed with one of Tom's relatives who lived on the outskirts of the town. Staying in the heart of town proved much more convenient.

Because of his two national titles, James's ranking had risen dramatically in a short time. Consequently, when we checked the draw at Kalamazoo, his name appeared as the second seed. Traditionally on the evening before play starts all the seeds line up on center court to be introduced. When James's name was announced, he heard the fifth seed Rafael DeMesa nudge the player next to him and say "Who's James Blake?"—probably voicing what many others were thinking. As it turned out, James played Rafael in the semifinals and beat him quite soundly. Those close to him as he came off the court might have heard him mutter, "Guess he knows who James Blake is now."

Mix It Up, Make It Nice

We discovered the final match is quite an event in Kalamazoo. On the day before, we were pleasantly surprised to receive an invitation to brunch on the morning of the match—quite a grand affair. The match itself played to a packed stadium—a reprise of the Clay Court final with Rudy Rake on the other side of the net. James played a nervous first set, which he lost at love, won the next but then lost the next two by identical scores of 6-4.

Nothing could dampen the excitement of that special day. Tom and I stood next to James for the trophy presentation. Tom could barely contain his pride in his youngest son. Both players made a speech, and we both became even prouder. James first thanked God for his talent and then his parents for nurturing that talent. One of the ushers told me in the many years she had listened to players' speeches this was the first that brought tears to her eyes.

Despite this last loss, James ended his junior years as the number-one player in the country—quite an accomplishment for a player from a cold-weather state who had been largely unheard of until his last two and a half years of play. It had all happened so fast we could hardly believe it. It surprised many of James's contemporaries and their parents, especially those who had routinely beaten him in earlier years.

At that time the USTA would give a wildcard entry into the US Open to the Kalamazoo champion. James missed out on that, but they gave him a wildcard into the qualifying rounds. Our youngest son was playing in the US Open. It seemed like a dream come true. Of course we went to watch him play, but the weather didn't cooperate. Twice we drove down but rain forced us to come back without seeing him play.

As a player, he could get a pass for us into the players' quarters. How exciting to walk around and know any minute you could bump into one of the legends of the game. You might see Pete Sampras eating lunch, Andre Agassi chatting with friends, Lindsay Davenport relaxing in the lounge. It all seemed new and wonderful to us.

When he did finally play we weren't there. Since it was still raining in Fairfield it seemed there would be no chance for him to get on the court, but it must have stopped long enough in the city for him to play. He split the first two sets with Laurence Tieleman, but couldn't hold on to the last set. The next day, *The New York Times* ran a photo of James with a lovely write-up about how much he admires Arthur Ashe.

So we missed the singles but Thomas's Harvard teammate Mike Pasarella made sure we didn't miss Thomas and James playing together in the doubles qualifier. He came into the club where I was working behind the desk and practically carried me out. "Your sons are playing in the US Open," he said. "Someone will take over the desk for you." We didn't stop to see if someone did. They played well together but lost a close match in a third-set tiebreaker. For both of them, just taking part in the US Open was a dream come true.

As the top player in the country, the USTA now invited James to several tournaments we never knew existed. First, he went to Canada to play in the Canadian Junior International where he drew one of the seeds in the first round. James lost the first set, 6-1. Despite the easy victory, his opponent complained loudly and often about how badly he was playing. Spurred by this perceived insult, James raised his level of play and won the next two sets, 6-3, 6-3.

This turned out to be the first of James's many encounters with Lleyton Hewitt.

A week later, James was thrilled to play for the first time in the US Open Junior Championships. He won his first round and then came up against the top seed, Daniel Elsner. He fought hard, but lost 7-6, 6-2.

The summer over, James now had to think about moving on to college. After his success in junior tennis he eagerly looked forward to joining his brother at Harvard, where he knew the challenges would be far greater, both in tennis and in academics, than any he had so far encountered.

Mix It Up, Make It Nice

You've got to jump off cliffs all the time
and build your wings on the way down.

—RAY BRADBURY

Chapter 7:
The Harvard Years

L IKE THOMAS, JAMES received his acceptance letter
from Harvard before Christmas of his senior year in
high school. Unlike Thomas, who had Harvard in his
sights since middle school, James was not sure whether
he wanted to attend.

Because of his success in his final two years of junior
tennis ending with the number-one ranking in the
country, James found himself bombarded with offers of
full scholarships to prestigious universities. He visited
several of these, notably North Carolina and Notre Dame,
and was tempted by both. North Carolina, largely because
of its most famous alumnus (James had virtually papered
his room with Michael Jordan posters), impressed him the

most. Besides offering him a substantial scholarship, James could not believe the treatment enjoyed by athletes at that school.

"They treat them like gods," he told us. "They go to tournaments in private planes—someone even does their laundry."

This was a far cry from the treatment he saw the number-one singles player on the Harvard tennis team (his brother Thomas) receive. At Harvard, all sports take a back seat to academics—a concept his father and I embraced heartily. However, despite the prospect of a life of luxury, after talking it over with his brother, his friends and us and after sizing up all the pros and cons, James decided to follow his brother to Harvard. The fact Thomas would be there to help him make the transition from high school to college played a large part in helping him to make up his mind. "It will be like having my best friend there," James told a local interviewer.

Thomas did help James enormously in that first year, just as he had when James became a freshman in high school. With no one to guide him, Thomas had found the transition to college life difficult, but James's path proved much easier because of his brother's prior experience. Thomas helped him, not only on the court but in the classroom as well, advising him on which courses to consider and which to leave alone. It made James's first year away from home a positive experience. Coach Dave Fish summed up Thomas's attitude: "Tommy brought James along wonderfully. They're very protective and watch out for each other." Thomas enjoyed his role. "I like watching out for him, making sure he doesn't make the same mistakes I made in my freshman year."

Tom and I were ecstatic James chose to attend Harvard. We had tried to be objective and not interfere with his decision, but I'm sure he knew what we, especially his father, wanted. We had many offers of free college tuition for both our sons, but the financial incentive proved not strong enough to lure Tom away from his desire for them to attend the best university in the country. We discussed finances briefly, but I believe we knew all along what we would do. It's hard to say no when Harvard says yes. It meant sacrificing some of our retirement funds, for Ivy League schools do not give athletic scholarships but weighing their future against our retirement made for a very easy decision.

James bonding with the Harvard tennis team
before he decided to go there

One of the "pros" that helped influence James's decision was he already knew all of the players on the Harvard tennis team, for he often came to Cambridge with us on weekends to watch the matches. Occasionally, he would stay over in Mather House (his brother's, and later his, dormitory) and socialize with Thomas and his friends, so he had experienced life at Harvard. He felt he had a good chance of playing on the team, possibly at the number-four singles position. One of the reasons he turned down an offer from Stanford was because he thought, with all of their stellar players—Paul Goldstein and the Bryan twins (all three outstanding junior players) among others, he would be relegated to the bench. He wanted to play, and he felt confident he would make the team if he chose Harvard. Another reason for shunning Stanford was he felt it was expected for the top junior tennis players to go there. "I don't always like doing what I'm expected to do," he explained.

In his first three years at Harvard, Thomas had acquitted himself well. Initially unsure of securing a spot on the team, he responded to Coach Dave Fish's confidence in placing him at the number-four singles position with a 22-8 record, ending his first year as the regional "Player to Watch." In his sophomore year, Fish elevated Thomas to number-one singles, where he stayed for the rest of his college years. He also received All-American honors as a sophomore by reaching the round of 16 at the NCAA Championships. We were not there to see this but I heard about it from James, who called me during my shift at the tennis club. Bursting with pride for his brother's achievement, he couldn't wait to share the news with me. After years of sibling rivalry they have become each other's greatest fan. Had I known this would happen perhaps those filial fights would have been easier to take. I should have tried to ignore them as Tom often advised me. As usual, his insight proved right.

The honors kept coming in Thomas's third year when he became an All-American in doubles (with Mitty Arnold) by reaching the semifinals at the NCAA Championships, a feat no Harvard team had accomplished for more than 50 years. Mitty who hails from Massachusetts had become acquainted with Thomas when they both played junior tournaments in New England. Attending the same university cemented a friendship that endures today. They often played as a doubles team in their early years on the pro circuit.

Thomas also claimed EITA Player and Sportsman of the Year honors, as well as being named the National ITA Player to Watch, and ended the year with a singles ranking of 30 in the nation.

At the beginning of 1997 he entered the Milwaukee Classic, a tournament in which he had lost in the first round the previous year. Just after he arrived in Milwaukee his grandmother died peacefully at age 99. Thomas had been particularly close to my mother in her more lucid days, possibly because she was so fond of him.

The Harvard Years

I had to decide if I should tell him right away or wait until he was no longer in the tournament. I thought of what she would want and knew what I had to do. "Play this one for Gran," I said to myself, and he did. Not only did he win the tournament, he came home with the Sportsmanship trophy as well. Gran would have been proud.

Coming into Harvard, James had no thoughts of displacing his brother from his singles position. He would have been happy to play anywhere on the team. Thomas had gained enormous respect from his coaches and his teammates. His impressive serve had earned him the nickname "Tommy Gun" or sometimes just "Gun." When James came on the scene, much smaller than his brother, perhaps it was inevitable he became known as "Squirt Gun."

Sidelined for his first few weeks with a shoulder injury, when James did begin playing, Coach Fish surprised him by starting him at number-two singles. As a freshman in high school, James had been confident he would take over the number-two position right away, but recognizing the greater challenges of college tennis and knowing and respecting the abilities of the other players on the team, James had no expectation of jumping into the number-two position here. Right away we had a reprise of the high school situation.

Tom and I became excited at the prospect of the year ahead, watching both boys on the same team, possibly with the added bonus of seeing them team up to play doubles, for in college tennis, unlike in high school, players can play both singles and doubles for the team. Robert Burns once made a well-known observation about "best laid schemes," and we had to acknowledge his superior wisdom, for the year didn't turn out quite the way we had anticipated.

James started late because of his injury and Thomas had an abbreviated season when he severely injured a hamstring early in his last year, but during the short time in between we enjoyed the camaraderie between them when they played doubles together, and also when they played singles on adjacent courts. An article in a Harvard publication entitled "Brotherhood at the Baseline" quotes Dave Fish on his view of the healthy competition between the two: "If they are playing on courts next to each other, there's an enormous energy charge flowing in both directions. If James is just going through somebody on the next court, watch Tom crank his game up; you can almost see him thinking, 'I'm not going to let junior finish before me.'"

At this time they also began to cause a stir in other publications. *USA Today* featured an article called "Double Promise" by Doug Smith, speculating both might eventually turn pro, *The Boston Globe* focused on how competitive they became over Nintendo games but in tennis they pulled for each other. Thomas is quoted as saying, "It's kind of annoying getting everyone I know asking, 'Who's better?' and 'Why's your little brother ranked ahead of you?' I'm happy for him. It doesn't bother me at all." That wasn't just for the press—he meant it.

My favorite piece appeared in the Boston Herald just after James decided to turn pro. Steve Buckley reports a conversation between Thomas and James, each accusing the other of starting the numerous fights they had growing up. "He would start the fights and then I would end up getting in trouble," claims Thomas. When asked if this were true, James comes back with, "No. And it has nothing to do with the fact that I have a really bad temper and like to get my way."

They were in Boston helping to promote a tennis tournament at Longwood Cricket Club in which both were playing. Asked what would happen if they ever played each other in a tournament, James said, "We'd both be very serious about winning, because it's professional tennis. But the beauty of it is that, when it was over, it would mean that one of us would be advancing. It would be good for the family. No matter what happens, we'd still be brothers when it was over. We'd still be friends." That kind of attitude is music to a mother's ears. Ironically, just a few months later that situation arose—almost.

In November 1998 they played in the Rolex Region I Championships in Philadelphia. It turned out to be one of the best college tournaments Tom and I ever watched. They played their first matches at different times, and we watched them win their way into the semifinals. Then the tournament officials put the two semifinal matches on at the same time. A raised viewing area separated the two courts and we had one son playing on each side. Tom and I tried to keep up with both matches, running from one side to the other and reporting to each other on their progress during the changeovers. During his match, Thomas severely bruised his heel and we thought he might have to stop. He played the last few games with abandon, going for big serves and winning shots, trying to keep the running to a minimum. The strategy worked. He eked out the match with a tie-break win in the third set, and James won his, so they were scheduled to play each other for the title on the following day.

First they had to play the doubles final. Although Thomas's foot still pained him, he didn't want to let his brother down. The injury hampered his movement and adversely affected his big weapon, his serve. Playing against another brother/brother senior/freshman doubles team, Adam and Aaron Marchetti, they dropped the first set, but turned it around in the next two and won 6-3, 6-1. However, the effort proved too much for Thomas. He had to default the singles scheduled for the same day.

"I would've liked to have played. It would have been fun since we never played in a tournament against each other before," Thomas said. "But it did make the decision not to play easier, knowing it was him and letting him have the win."

We were all disappointed, including Thomas and James. I think James's prediction would have proved true. Although it was not a professional match, they would have played at a highly competitive level but with no trace of animosity before, during or after the match. It would have been a good match to watch.

"I'm sure we would have had a good match, but he is probably a little more experienced than me at this point," James conceded. "But maybe sometime down the road we'll get another chance." Strangely enough, though they often played in the same tournaments during their first years on the professional tour, they never had to play each other again.

James ended his freshman tennis year with a college ranking of 14. At one point he had ranked as high as 3 in singles. He became the first Harvard freshman to be named an All-American and only the 10th in Harvard history to achieve that honor. With his meteoric rise in the rankings, there was much speculation about his leaving college and going out on the professional tour with his brother. Tom and I read a few articles about this but paid scant attention to them, for at this point we still thought James would stay until graduation. I recall being mystified when I heard the Princeton coach, watching James play a college match in his freshman year, remark Fish wouldn't have him for long. I didn't know what he meant.

On June 4 1998 Thomas received his Harvard diploma. What a glorious day that was for Tom and me. I cried and Tom beamed with pride as we watched our 6'5" oldest son parade to the podium in his cap and gown, but the warmth we felt inside was not enough to offset the chill of the day. It must have been one of the coldest June 4ths in Massachusetts's history. I recall sitting on the grounds of Mather House, unable to control my chattering teeth despite wearing a long-sleeved shirt with a thick sweater over it. Thomas, still basking in the warm glow of graduation, barely noticed the temperature, but James, seeing how cold I looked, told him to go up to his room and get a jacket for me.

After graduation the whole family traveled to Texas to see Thomas receive the Thomas McGill Scholar/Athlete award. Both boys had been named to the USTA All-American Summer Team, which held its first practice sessions in the same town, so Tom and I stayed an extra day to watch them. After that, we went home, leaving them to test their skills on a professional level.

They both played several Futures tournaments (the minor leagues of professional tennis), and felt somewhat encouraged by their results. They found they could compete with others at the same level, and James reached the semifinals of a tournament in Waco and the quarters in another. Even with the prospect of a wildcard entry into the qualifiers of the Pilot Pen tournament in New Haven Connecticut and the US Open in August, he decided he wasn't ready for the tour yet, and opted for at least one more year at Harvard.

"I didn't think I was ready to handle the pressure of being on the pro tour this summer," said James. "I need to get a little stronger and physically in better shape. I just need to get experience and play a lot of matches." His junior coach Brian Barker and his Harvard coach Dave Fish both applauded James's maturity in making this decision. "I think James understands tennis and life in general more than most kids his age," commented Brian.

At the Pilot Pen tournament he lost a close three-set match, and might have pulled it out if he hadn't experienced severe leg cramps in the final set. He won his first two rounds at the US Open Qualifiers but lost in two sets to David Wheaton, a much more experienced player, in the final match. Had he made it into the main draw it might have made him think again about his decision to return to Harvard.

Going back for his sophomore year proved a good choice for several reasons. I'm sure James would agree with that. I believe when he looks back that second year at Harvard will stand out as one of the more memorable of his young life. Several more news articles appeared, the majority applauding his decision, but also predicting this would likely be his last year of college tennis. Finally, Tom and I had to face the fact we might have to defer seeing our youngest receive his diploma.

James chose to sit out the National Clay Court Championships, the first leg of the college grand slam, in September. He needed some rest from tennis after his grueling summer on the pro circuit. He also needed to spend some time on his schoolwork. By October, he felt ready to compete again.

He traveled to Austin Texas for the second leg of the slam, the All-America Championships. That weekend,

Mix It Up, Make It Nice

October 19-20, saw torrential rains bombard Texas, forcing long delays in tournament scheduling. At one point the Harvard contingent had to abandon their car and they watched it float away. Because of the weather the tournament had to be extended an extra day. On Monday the 21st the semis and finals moved indoors. The only player left in both singles and doubles, James prepared for a long, tough day of tennis. His first opponent in singles, Ryan Wolters, a senior from Stanford, had won this tournament as a freshman. James broke his serve at 5-6 to set up a tiebreaker, which he won, 7-2. He then took the second set, 6-4. Then he played Ryan Sachire for the title. Ryan, one year ahead of James in their junior years, had beaten James in Boston at the Junior National Indoor Championships. Ryan had been the heavy favorite, but James had surprised us all by taking him to three sets. Now it was James's turn. He jumped out to a 6-3 win in the opening set, but had to play another tiebreaker to win the match and the title. Again he made history by becoming the first Ivy League player ever to win a Grand Slam title.

James had little time to savor his victory. After a short rest, he was ready to play the doubles semifinal with his partner, Kunj Majmudar. Kunj had taken Thomas's place as James's doubles partner after Thomas graduated. One year ahead of James, Kunj managed to juggle tennis and studies admirably. Eventually he graduated *summa cum laude* and now works in Boston. Part of the J-Block, he still supports his doubles partner at most of the more important tournaments.

James and Kunj dropped the first set quickly at 6-2, but then found some reserves of strength and took the next two sets in tiebreakers. In the final set they saved three match points to force the tiebreak and then proceeded to lose five of the first seven points. Down 4-6, they faced two more match points. Again they rallied with three points in a row and finally sealed the victory at 9-7. These long matches had taken up most of the day, but the tournament, already a day behind schedule, had to go on.

The Harvard Years

In the last match of the day they competed against a duo from Illinois. The first set turned into an epic battle, which Harvard lost in an 11-9 tiebreaker. After the match, James conceded, "Last year with less experience I might have let go at that point." I'm sure no one would have faulted him if he had, but the team rallied once more and took the next set, 6-3. The final set went back and forth with three breaks of serve and Harvard squeaked it out at 7-5.

By the time they hit the last ball it was well into the next day. James, understandably in a euphoric state, didn't consider the time. Our phone rang around 3 a.m., and at first Tom and I feared the worst. Who calls at that hour? It must be bad news. Tom reached for the phone, and then a huge smile broke over his face. When he finally handed the phone to me, James willingly repeated the story for my benefit. I believe for that day alone he felt justified in his decision to go back to Harvard for one more year.

During the Christmas break James and Thomas played a Futures tournament in Florida. Thomas reached the quarters, but James turned a few heads when he won the tournament. At that point I don't believe Tom and I realized what our youngest son had accomplished. The pro circuit still remained a mystery to us, and just as we had learned earlier about the system in New England tennis, we now needed an education in professional tennis and the relative importance of Futures, Satellites and the like. After receiving several congratulatory phone calls from people who were beginning to take a serious interest in James, we began to believe perhaps he could have the career in tennis, which up to now had been only a dream.

The dream had to be deferred while James concentrated on the second half of the year in college tennis. In February he competed in the third leg of the collegiate grand slam, the Rolex National Indoor Championships held in Dallas. At the time Tom's cousin lived there so we made the trip to watch James play and to spend some time with Cissie and her family. He made the trip worthwhile by winning a hard-fought final match against Robert Kendrick to take his second title. Coincidentally, he played this match in the same club and against the same opponent as in his first junior national victory, the 18s Indoors.

James and Tom had enjoyed Cissie's hospitality during that junior tournament too. Cissie and Tom had played together as children and still enjoyed each other's company. She has a son, Randy, a few years older than James. Randy and James became firm friends at that time and Randy still loudly supports James whenever he goes to one of his tournaments.

At this point James had still not totally made up his mind to leave Harvard, but his father and I had already become resigned to the fact this would probably be his last year for a while.

"People want to know which way I'm leaning," said James, "but I'm not really sure yet. I'll make the decision early in the summer, after the NCAAs."

With only three singles losses during the entire year, James became the heavy favorite to win this last leg of the collegiate grand slam. Tom and I went to Athens Georgia to watch him compete. Day after broiling day, we watched him handle the pressure that goes with being the top seed and win his way into the finals. As James said, "It's pretty tough when you're number one, because you don't have anything to prove. All the guys are looking to knock you off. You have to find something to push you to win, to push you to be even more competitive."

For the first time in more than two decades the two top seeds were set to compete in the final match. After splitting the first two sets with his good friend Jeff Morrison, James found himself on the wrong end of a 5-2 score in the final set. He held serve and then broke Jeff in the next game to put the match back on serve, but Jeff was not to be denied. James relaxed slightly after getting the match back on serve and Jeff took advantage, coming up with some big shots to break back and take the championship.

The Harvard Years

Despite the loss, James retained his number-one college ranking with an astounding 41-4 win/loss record for the year. Once again he made Harvard history by becoming its first number-one player. He now decided to do what many had predicted, and leave academia for the pro tennis circuit.

"I'll miss my friends at school and the whole atmosphere at Harvard," he said. But I realized that to improve at the rate I'd like to, I need to play with players who can push me in practice. I didn't feel I could get that in college."

Towards the end of James's second year at Harvard we began to realize what an incredibly smart decision he had made in going back for another year. Because of the outstanding year he had enjoyed in the college ranks coupled with his early successes in the few pro matches he had played, sports agents began to show great interest. I would come home from work to see the light blinking furiously on the message machine. Every day we listened to three or four agents promising to make our youngest son a millionaire.

Tom and I didn't know what to make of it. We agreed to meet with some of them. When they threw astronomical figures at us, Tom and I just looked at each other, uncomprehending, not even knowing how to ask intelligent questions. This was new ground for us. It all sounded much too good to be true, so of course we remained skeptical. Once again Brian came to the rescue. He arranged a breakfast meeting in Cambridge with James, Tom and me, and Mats Wilander, a former number-one player on the pro tour and Brian's friend, whose advice proved invaluable.

The agent from IMG, Carlos Fleming, who came to Harvard to watch James play, had impressed us both. A top-ranked player at the University of Kansas, Carlos tried a brief stint on the pro circuit. After he hung up his rackets, he began working with IMG and has risen to become a vice-president in that company. We felt he, more than some of the other agents who talked with us, would work hard in James's best interest. Mats also added his seal of approval and that was all we needed to hear. It proved a good choice for Carlos almost immediately procured contracts for both Thomas and James with Nike and Dunlop.

As an added bonus, what began as a business arrangement in 1999 has developed into a relationship that will endure long after James stops playing professionally and Carlos stops being his agent. He has become a firm friend, not only to James but also to our whole family. "I couldn't have chosen a better agent than Carlos," said James. "He's legitimately one of my best friends."

As predicted, James then said goodbye to the comforts of college life and college tennis and embarked on a new career. Several times during the next two years he may have questioned his decision. He found life on the pro tour a lot more difficult than he had envisioned it.

If at first you don't succeed, try try again.

—attributed to ROBERT THE BRUCE, KING OF SCOTS,
14th century

Chapter 8:
Testing the Waters

I'M NOT SURE WHAT Tom and I expected when James left Harvard to pursue a career in tennis. We had no qualms when Thomas went out on the circuit. With his Harvard diploma in hand, we felt his future was assured and he could take a year or two off before settling down to reality. However James was about to leave Harvard in search of what we still believed was only a dream. Bewildered by the many different agents and coaches who seemed to think he might make it, we grudgingly agreed it was worth a try.

I don't think we believed all the "pie in the sky" predictions with which they bombarded us, but Tom realized James seemed anxious to try it so we agreed to let him cut short his education with the assurance he could go back to Harvard at any time if the new career didn't work out. This played an important part in James's decision. Realistic enough to realize an athlete's career could be tenuous, he wanted something solid to fall back on. "Harvard is great that way," he told one reporter. "I could leave for as long as I wanted to, and still be welcomed back to finish." Yet there remained a tinge of regret. "It was difficult walking away from Harvard," he said. "I miss the whole atmosphere. I had so many close friends around me."

James had moved with unexpected ease from junior into college tennis, despite several warnings from tennis players already in college about the huge difference in the level of play, but he had few illusions about the transition into pro tennis. Yet again he benefited from his brother's prior experience. Thomas had been playing on the circuit for a year and gave him some idea of what to expect. During their high school and college years they had become used to winning. Thomas warned James it's hard out there. He told him his biggest adjustment would be learning how to lose—he would play against talented young players from all over the world who played for more than glory. They had a powerful added incentive; they played for their livelihood.

Even though Thomas warned James about the level of competition, I don't think he was prepared to lose quite as much as he did. For a long stretch in that first year he lost in the first round of every tournament he played. It would have been no surprise to us if he had abandoned the dream and decided to go back to the comforts of college life, but as long as he felt he was improving, albeit ever so slightly, James wanted to continue. In his junior days his father often told him not to worry about the wins, just think about getting better. At the time James refused to accept this premise but now he began to see the wisdom behind it.

Brian once observed if James thought hitting forehands for 10 hours a day would make his forehand 1 percent better, then he'd hit forehands for 10 hours a day.

Testing the Waters

This attitude, and the work ethic we had tried to instill in him, made him stay with it. Tom used to tell his sons you can't control your level of talent, but you can control your level of effort. He urged them to put their best effort into anything they attempted—something he did regularly. James determined to be the best he could possibly be, and eventually his hard work paid dividends we could never have imagined.

I often wonder if most tennis fans have any idea how difficult it is for a young player to achieve a ranking on the pro tour. Just as we had to learn how the junior and college ranking systems worked, we now had to learn the ranking system on the professional level, which turned out to be quite different. Tom and I were amazed when we began to understand the complex system of points and how to attain them. After 10 years I still need Thomas to explain the finer points of the system. A youngster who has done well as a junior and feels he could make it on the tour might play for years in the "minor leagues" without receiving a single ranking point.

I'll attempt an explanation. There are three levels of tournament play. You begin with Futures, hope to work up to Challengers, and from there get into main ATP tournaments, where you finally acquire some recognition as well as more points and more money. Each tournament has a qualifying draw; some have pre-qualifying rounds. To achieve your first points on the ranking scale you must first get into a Futures tournament by winning three rounds in the 128-player qualifying draw. If you then win your first round in the main event, you earn one ranking point. Hallelujah! You've made it onto the computer. It's sort of a "Catch-22," for if you have no ranking, you have no guarantee of even getting into the qualifying rounds, preference always going to ranked players.

One day after Thomas and James had played and lost their first doubles match at the US Open, from my post behind the desk at the tennis club I heard a group of elderly ladies discussing the match and implying they thought the Blakes should have done better. Incensed, a mother defending her young, I stood up and asked if they

111

had any idea what it took to be in a position to even play in the US Open. I was heatedly telling them how proud I was of my sons' performance when, fortunately, the owner of the club came by, smoothed my ruffled feathers, then proceeded to placate his customers.

One way to bypass the qualifying tournament is to apply for a wildcard into the main event. Because of our sons' achievements at Harvard and with the help of their agent, Carlos Fleming, they obtained several wildcards, both in singles and doubles, into various Futures and Challenger events. However to continue to earn these wildcards you must prove yourself worthy of them by winning at least a first-round match.

When our two sons began playing on the professional circuit we found ourselves at a loss to understand this system. Thinking it would be similar to the junior ranking system, I recall how excited we were when James after about a year on the tour had a win over Paradorn Srichaphan, Thailand's number-one player whose ranking was much higher than his. In junior tennis if you beat a player ranked higher than you it did wonders for your ranking. "That should get him a few points," I said to Brian. Apparently not.

Brian tried to explain the system to us. Because the win over Paradorn came in the first round, it garnered only a few points. To make a dent in your ranking you have to go deep into a tournament. The minor tournaments offer substantially fewer points than the majors. A victory in a Futures tournament gives you the same number of points you would get if you win only three rounds in a higher contest, so for several reasons it's good to make it to the big time.

Our sons fared better than most young players starting out on the tour because they had the benefit of Carlos, who had negotiated deals with Nike and Dunlop for them. Free clothing and equipment went a long way towards easing the financial burden. Carlos also worked hard at procuring wildcards for them. This is where James's decision to delay turning pro for that extra year paid off. Had he opted for the tour after his first year, the endorsements and the benefits that go with them would not have been there.

During the years when Thomas and James played Futures and Challengers Tom and I had our own lives to live and while we enjoyed taking time off to watch our children play we couldn't manage it too often. We followed their results as much as possible but with tennis, especially the minor tournaments, getting short shrift in the sports news, it was not easy. After the first excitement of having them out on the tour, it seemed to settle into a regular job for both of them. I recall one customer at the club where I worked who followed their careers much closer than we did. He would come into the club and tell me which tournaments they had played, which they were going to play and what were their current rankings. "You know more about my children than I do," I told him.

In 2006 the people at Roland Garros compiled a booklet for each player at the French Open that year, tracing his entire tennis career. This booklet has proved invaluable in jogging my memory of those first years. Thumbing through it, I was amazed at how few wins James enjoyed in his early career. With results like that no one would have faulted him for giving up. I believe his coach Brian Barker had a lot to do with James's perseverance. Brian has a wonderful optimistic philosophy, which has helped us all through some difficult situations, but even with his optimism none of us could have predicted what the future held for James.

I'm still amazed considering all the obstacles in his way James became one of the top 10 players in the world and stayed in that lofty position for three years. Most players will admit it's easier to get there than to stay there, because when you're coming up there is much less pressure from yourself and from the media.

I have little patience with sports writers who criticize James for never winning a major title. If James never wins another match I will still be enormously proud of him for what he has accomplished, mainly through hard work and determination—values instilled in him by his father. James was never the infant prodigy expected to make it on the pro tour. We didn't spend a ton of money on tennis lessons. He didn't leave home and family at an early age to pursue some nebulous career. In fact as an undersized teenager forced to wear a full-body brace for 18 hours each day, few would have predicted his eventual success. One of his doctors commenting on that success remarked technically it shouldn't have happened. He may have dreamed of a career in tennis, but we (including James) had no inkling of it becoming a reality until he began to do well in his first two years in college.

Without that booklet from the French Open, I would have remembered few of those early tournaments. Unfortunately I have no such booklet chronicling Thomas's career. What I recall of his six years on the pro tour is they were punctuated with numerous injuries, mainly the chronic back problems that had bothered him during his junior years, but also a wrist injury requiring surgery that kept him out for more than a year. After attaining a ranking in the top 300, the injuries got the better of him and in 2005 he abandoned the cycle of injury, rehab, then trying to recover the lost points.

Commenting on Thomas leaving the pro tour, James said, "He tried it, didn't quite make it, but he had fun, has a lot of great stories, and now he's not stressed. He's going to go into the real world and there's nothing wrong with that—that's what 99 percent of the world does." Obviously it was not such a big deal to either of them as the media would like to make it.

While on the tour Thomas made many friends and earned a lot of respect. Still in the tennis world he often travels with James when Brian needs some time off, has traveled as hitting partner with one of the top women pros, and more recently became head coach of the Washington Kastles, one of the nine teams that play Team Tennis in July.

Thomas and James played in two Futures tournaments in Canada in June 1999, just after James turned pro. They did well in the first with James reaching the semifinals so Tom and I drove to Montreal to watch the second and spend some time with our boys. What I recall most about that week is the unusually hot weather and the prodigious amounts of food our sons consumed. During their college years their appetites had increased considerably, and their current line of work necessitated even more calories. I also remember James won the tournament in an exciting three-set final in which he lost the first set but came back to win the next two. His opponent had beaten Thomas in the semifinals, once again dashing our hopes for a chance to see them play each other.

After that victory, the future started to look even brighter when James received a wildcard into the grass court tournament in Newport Rhode Island, one of the main ATP tournaments. He drew one of his idols, MaliVai Washington, a former top-10 player, in the first round and after a shaky start regrouped and won in the final two sets, giving him his first tour win. Meanwhile, Thomas, playing in the qualifying rounds, notched a win over David Wheaton, another well-known name in the tennis world, to put him into the main draw. All too soon, the bubble burst. James lost in the next round, and Thomas in his first round in the main draw.

After that they went back to the Challengers, first to Winnetka Illinois. Neither did well in the singles there, but together they brought home the doubles trophy and a very welcome check. One of Thomas's Harvard friends lived in Winnetka at that time, and she and her family watched all their matches. I would get a telephone report each time they played, detailing their progress.

With his ranking still not high enough for entry into Challenger events, James often had to play the qualifying rounds. After failing to qualify in Lexington he went on to Binghamton NY, where he won his three qualifying matches, then won three main draw matches to take him to the semifinals. He played this match on a weekend so we drove up to watch. He won the first set but couldn't maintain the same level of play in the next two and lost in the third to Anthony Dupuis, an older, much more experienced player. Nevertheless, going deep into the tournament moved his ranking up considerably.

Mix It Up, Make It Nice

He received wildcards into two tour events in Washington DC and Boston, but lost in the first rounds. Then, courtesy of a wildcard, he played for the first time in the main draw of the US Open. After this match, which he lost badly to Chris Woodruff, 6-2, 6-2, 6-1, James realized he wasn't yet ready to play at that level. At the time James was ranked 333 in the world, while Woodruff, ranked at 71, had been as high as 25. After the match, James said he hoped getting beaten so badly would spur him on to go the extra mile. Thoughtfully analyzing his effort, he said, "I think part of the extra mile of not getting beat like this again, is getting beat like this a few more times. That makes you work a little harder. That makes you want to get back there a little more. That makes you a little hungrier."

After that match he did get beaten a few more times. In fact he couldn't string together a series of wins until November 1999, when he won two Futures tournaments in succession, the second of these ending in a third-set tiebreaker.

These successes at the end of the year helped raise James's ranking and encouraged him to continue. He began the year 2000, his first full year as a pro player, with high hopes.

The year commenced on a high note when Justin Gimelstob withdrew from the Hopman Cup and the USTA asked James to replace him. For a young player with only six months' experience on the tour, this was a tremendous honor. His first chance to play for his country, James could hardly contain his excitement.

Sponsored by the International Tennis Federation, the Hopman Cup is an annual event played in Perth Australia. It involves eight teams from different countries competing for the ultimate prize. Each team consists of one male and one female player. They divide the eight competitors into two groups, then each team plays against the other three in his group. The winners of each group then compete for the trophy. The format is one men's singles match, one women's singles match and then the players team up for mixed doubles, which often proves the deciding point.

Testing the Waters

Besides the glory of winning for your country, each winning player brings home a platinum gold tennis ball encrusted with diamonds as well as some Australian dollars.

We were planning to celebrate two birthdays, James on December 28 and Thomas on December 29, when James received the call. Birthdays were forgotten in the whirlwind of finding James's passport, getting him packed and sending him off "down under." Luck was with him, for it snowed heavily on the day he left and his plane was one of the few to take off that day. Australia is 16 hours ahead of us, and the tournament began on January 1, so he had no time to spare. He must have played his first match with some serious jet lag.

James lost his first two matches, against Jonas Björkman and Xavier Malisse, but was able to notch a two-set win over Wayne Ferreira, a player with a ranking much higher than his. Although this did nothing for his ranking, it made him think maybe he could compete with some of the big players.

A win like that should have made his confidence soar. Yet in the next few months he had many more losses than wins. Going through the log of his accomplishments provided by the French Open, you see many first-round losses, punctuated by an occasional win, with another loss right after it. It must have been disheartening to travel to so many different parts of the country only to lose in the first round and have to try your luck somewhere else. Many of his losses were heartbreakingly close, and perhaps this helped to make him stay the course—he felt he was still improving.

Tom and I made a trip to Florida in March 2000. James was playing in the qualies of a Masters event in Miami. The eight Masters tournaments are just a little less important than the four Slams, providing more points than regular ATP events, so they attract all the top players. Our main reason for this trip was to see the living conditions our boys enjoyed in their new home in Tampa. We were pleasantly surprised by their spacious, tastefully furnished two-bedroom apartment. We found out later we could thank Kevin O'Connor, the manager at the Saddlebrook tennis complex, for his help in setting them up.

After checking a few practice sites, they had chosen Tampa and Saddlebrook for their home base. Kevin had taken them under his wing and helped enormously with their living arrangements. We were grateful to Kevin for helping two unknown players just starting out on the tour. James's eventual success has helped to pay him back, in the young players who choose Saddlebrook because of James's involvement with it.

After a few days in Tampa we drove to Miami to watch James play. He drew Wayne Arthurs, an experienced, big-serving player, in the first round. He lost the first set, then dug in and won the second at 7-5. The third set kept us on the edge of our seats until James succumbed in a tiebreaker. He came so close, but it just goes down in the books as another first-round loss—another heartbreaker.

His fortunes improved little over the next few months. He suffered many losses, with now and then a lone win, with a loss right after it. In July, however, he had a positive experience when he played Team Tennis with Hartford's new team, the Fox Force. In April Thomas and James had been recruited for the team and they were excited about playing so close to home. (Hartford is an hour's drive from Fairfield.) Tom and I again looked forward to seeing them play together, but again our hopes were dashed when Thomas needed an operation on his wrist.

Founded in 1974, World Team Tennis comprises nine teams that play for three weeks in July. A completely different concept, teams play just one set each of men's singles, women's singles, men's doubles, women's doubles, and mixed doubles. In contrast to the complete quiet of a conventional tennis match, Team Tennis encourages noisy audience participation. Players recruited for the teams are often youngsters (like Thomas and James) just beginning their careers. Most teams will also recruit a well-known player (a "marquee player") who typically will play a limited schedule. Even without his brother, James enjoyed the experience, and at the end of the three weeks they named him "Rookie of the Year," which brought prestige as well as an extra paycheck. Several years after that first experience, James has been in demand as the "marquee player."

Returning to the tour he suffered a few more losses, but in September he strung together five wins in Houston and attained his first Challenger trophy. The two final matches were edge-of-the-seat affairs involving three close tiebreakers. In November a victory in another Challenger event helped to dispel his earlier frustrations. He was finally beginning to move up in the rankings.

James began the year 2001 with a loss in the final round of the Australian Open qualifiers. He then entered a Challenger tournament in Hawaii. He posted some good wins, but lost the final match in three sets to Andy Roddick. He followed this with a depressing run of losses in qualifying tournaments until the end of April when he qualified for an ATP tournament in Houston and won his first round against Christophe Rochus, only to lose in the next round. At this point I could imagine he might have questioned his career choice.

After reaching the finals of another Challenger event in May he had another series of losses, but in July, again at the Newport grass court tournament, he achieved his first real breakthrough. In the first round he rallied from a set down to beat the top seed, Vladimir Voltchkov. He then proceeded to win two more matches, taking him to the semifinals. An ATP tournament, this gave him a lot of points and did wonders for his ranking.

I should mention up to this time Brian his coach had traveled only sporadically with him. Beginning with the Newport tournament he became a full-time coach, which had an enormous impact on James's career. Until this time James had had little success against well-known players in the game.

I recall the time Brian made this decision. Sometimes overly cautious, he was reluctant to leave his position as Head of Junior Tennis at The Tennis Club of Trumbull.

Mix It Up, Make It Nice

One day he came into the club while I was working behind the desk. When he pulled up the other chair I guessed he had something momentous to discuss. "I've decided to travel with James," he told me. Registering less surprise than he expected, I asked, "What took you so long?"

Less than one month after Brian joined him on tour, as a wildcard entry into a Masters tournament in Cincinnati James registered a win over Arnaud Clement, a top-20 player. In the next round of that tournament he had to play Patrick Rafter, and although James lost, this match along with Patrick's gracious comments helped bolster James's confidence. James had lost the first set in a 9-7 tie-breaker, but failed to play at the same level in the next set, losing it 6-2. As they shook hands, Rafter asked him if he now believed he could beat someone like him, implying the only reason for James's loss was he didn't believe in himself. That gave James something to think about, and may have proved a turning point in his career.

Not long after, James won for the first time in the main draw of the US Open, his favorite tournament. Entering the tournament as a wildcard, he played his match on one of the small outer courts, but nothing could blunt the enormous thrill of posting his first singles victory at the US Open—the culmination of a childhood dream. Now he felt he belonged on the circuit.

Although James lost his next match, it served to catapult him into the public eye. After losing the first set to Lleyton Hewitt, the fourth seed, he conquered his nerves, and playing inspired tennis proceeded to win the next two. During the third set a linesman twice called a foot fault on Hewitt. Hewitt exploded with rage, and appealed to the chair umpire. "Look at him, mate," indicating the linesman (an African American), "Then look at him," pointing at his opponent. "You tell me what the similarity is."

The umpire had the offending linesman removed but Hewitt's words had been picked up by the microphone and this turned into a *cause célèbre*. After winning the third set, James's legs began to cramp. The trainer gave him medication to help, but he may have swallowed it too quickly because he then threw up on one of the changeovers. In the hot, humid weather conditions, the cramps worsened, and although James fought gamely the fifth set was virtually over before it began.

Sitting in the front row of Louis Armstrong Stadium, I could tell James was in pain and I wanted him to retire. Tom assured me he wouldn't, and apparently knew his son only too well. "Knowing my son, I knew he'd try to finish," he told the press. Ignoring the win/loss factor as he often did, he also said, "Total elation and happiness for him; he's playing super tennis." His coach echoed that sentiment, telling James, "If you keep playing like that, you're going to win—a lot."

After the match Tom and I sat with James as they pumped fluids into him to relieve dehydration. When we finally emerged we were bombarded by cameras and reporters, querying us about Hewitt's remarks concerning the Black linesman. Worried about James's health issues we had paid little attention. Now they forced us to address the issue. "Do your think Hewitt's remarks were racist?" one reporter asked me. I didn't know what Hewitt had said so I asked the reporter to repeat the remarks for me. I turned his question back on him. "What do you think?" I asked him. To me, the answer seemed all too obvious.

We were amazed by the furor caused by this incident. All the papers next day were filled with it. A huge picture of James appeared on the front page of *The New York Times* Sports section, as well as in the London *Times.* James had to attend numerous press conferences. Instead of taking offence he gave Lleyton the benefit of the doubt, said it was in the heat of the moment and largely dismissed it. Many of the greats of the tennis world—Pete Sampras, Andre Agassi—applauded James's demeanor. "We can focus on the negative if you want," said Agassi, "but I think he set an example about dignity and class and tolerance. I think it's something everybody can learn from." That may have been the start of the deep friendship James and Andre enjoy today.

One reporter applauded James's stand, and compared him to Arthur Ashe, which James considered a huge compliment. Many years ago, Arthur had defused a blatantly insensitive, racist comment from Ilie Năstase during a tennis match with a mild "That's unfortunate." James had a similar reaction: "I won't dwell on it. I'd just rather not get into it. I wouldn't say I completely ignore racial issues ... I do try to give people the benefit of the doubt and think the best of them."

Other reporters, looking for a bigger story (that is their job, so I can't fault them too much), labeled James an "Uncle Tom" and tried to goad him into providing them with a media circus. James refused to oblige. He accepted Hewitt's apology, saying if he had voiced such thoughts deliberately he might not have been so forgiving.

Getting nowhere with James, those reporters appealed to us. During the changeover of a doubles match we were watching someone thrust a piece of paper into Tom's hand. It said after conducting an investigation the tennis authorities had decided "the evidence was inconclusive as to the intent of Mr. Hewitt's remarks to the chair umpire." They would take no action against him. As we left the match, they had their microphones ready, anticipating our indignation. We told them guided by James we too would take the high road. They went away without a story. I have always firmly believed in the proverb "A soft answer turneth away wrath." This incident proved it works.

So in a strange twist of circumstance, while losing a match, James, a largely unknown tennis player, suddenly became something of a celebrity. Before long he became known for his successes on the tennis court, which proved much more to his liking.

Movin' on up ...

—Theme from *THE JEFFERSONS*

Chapter 9:
Perseverance Pays Off

SOON AFTER THE US Open ended that year, our nation forgot about tennis along with all other sports in the massive trauma of September 11. Sporting events along with events in most other areas were delayed while our nation grappled with its grief.

At the end of September with that disaster still all too fresh in our minds, James and Brian left for two ATP tournaments in China. Knowing how concerned I was about the long flight, James called as soon as they arrived. "Just thought you'd like to know we got here," he said, as I heaved an enormous sigh of relief.

Mix It Up, Make It Nice

James's ranking had now risen into the top 100 and he no longer needed a wildcard for some of the major tournaments. Still a long way from being seeded, he often had to play some of the best players in the world in the early rounds. In Hong Kong he drew Michael Chang as his first opponent. Although it was a close match—7-6, 7-5—it still went down as a first-round loss. Moving on to Tokyo, James posted some of the best results of his career with wins over Wayne Arthurs, Jonas Björkman and Marcelo Ríos, all of whom held rankings much higher than his. He lost in the semifinal to Hewitt but was thrilled with his performance at this tournament. He called again after the Ríos match and could hardly contain his excitement. He was moving up in the rankings, but more important, he saw his hard work paying off as his game improved.

The good news continued when he came home and received a call from Patrick McEnroe, the Davis Cup captain, who invited James to Winston-Salem to practice with the team. Because the US had lost in the first round at the beginning of the year, they now had to play a preliminary match with India to qualify to play the event in 2002. At the end of the week an excited James called me again. "Mom, I'm going to play," he told me. "Patrick has chosen me instead of Todd (Martin)."

Todd Martin, almost 10 years older than James, already had nine years' experience on the pro tour when the two met in 1999. In that year, Todd enjoyed his greatest success, attaining his highest ranking of number four in the world and reaching the finals of the US Open. Like James, Todd had attended college, Northwestern University, for two years before turning pro.

Todd had taken James under his wing from the days when James, still a sophomore at Harvard, had been a hitting partner with the Davis Cup team in 1999, the 100th anniversary of the event. The Cup originated at Harvard so it seemed fitting to hold the centennial in Boston and invite James, the first number-one college player in Harvard's history. Todd, a veteran Davis Cup player, was on the team again that year. He became James's mentor when he went on tour later that year, and

Perseverance Pays Off

in James's words, has helped him with "just about everything." Firm friends as well as sometime doubles partners, they have a tremendous admiration for each other. I believe Todd was almost as happy as James with Patrick's decision.

The event had been scheduled for September but was delayed until October because of the 9/11 tragedy. Knowing how much it meant to James to play for his country, Tom and I traveled to Winston-Salem to watch the matches. I often had to convince Tom we should seize the moment to watch our sons play, reminding him we could never be sure how long their careers would last. An extremely dedicated 3M employee, he balked at taking too much time off work. Because Davis Cup matches always take place on weekends we only needed to take Friday off, which made it easier to talk him into going.

The Davis Cup format consists of four players from each of the participating countries. The venue alternates between home and away, and is decided by where the match was played the previous year. Playing at home is a huge advantage because the home players choose either their favorite surface or one that has proved difficult for their opponents. On the first day (Friday), the two number-one singles players compete against the respective number-two players from the opposing team. Each match is three out of five sets so it often turns into a long day of tennis. Saturday is much shorter with just one doubles match. Sunday is the reverse singles, with the number-one and number-two players from each team playing against each other. As soon as one team wins three matches any remaining matches become "dead rubbers" which must be played, but in the shorter form of two out of three sets.

Andy Roddick, our number-one player, had won his match over young Harsh Mankad when James went on the court to play Leander Paes, India's number-one player. Paes, a Davis Cup veteran, felt he could take advantage of James's first-time jitters but James surprised him and a lot of others by taking the match in three sets. After eking out the first set at 7-5, James looked ready to fold in the second. Paes had broken James's serve, and held a 40-love lead on his own serve, one point away from going ahead by two games. James bore down, got the game back to deuce, and then proceeded to win it. That seemed to be the turning point for Paes. James won that set and the third, both by scores of 6-3.

Talking to us after the match James almost seemed at a loss to describe the emotions he went through on the court. "It's a whole different thing to play for your country," he said. "The first time you hear "Advantage USA" instead of "Advantage Blake," you realize there's a lot more at stake than in an individual tennis match." He said it almost amounted to a surreal experience playing in front of a crowd chanting "USA, USA."

Although this was only a preliminary match, it turned into one of the highlights of James's career. Patrick McEnroe had taken a huge risk in selecting James to play and James was elated he could fulfill Patrick's expectations. The victory meant Team USA now had qualified to play in the 2002 Davis Cup competition.

The first round took place in Oklahoma City and pitted the US against the Slovak Republic. Pete Sampras had joined the team so we knew James would only be used in the doubles competition, but Tom and I had so enjoyed our first taste of Davis Cup competition we decided to make the trip.

The atmosphere at Davis Cup matches is vastly different from other tennis matches. In the opening ceremonies the players on each team are introduced individually amid loud applause. Then each team stands for the national anthems of the countries involved—a moving experience for everyone, especially the players.

When play begins the crowd gets into the action, cheering loudly for their country. A contingent of US fans who call themselves the "Netheads" come equipped with a brass band and a store of chants for each player. Always respecting tennis etiquette they only perform between points. Often the audience enjoys acrobatic displays, juggling acts and the like during changeovers. It seems more like a football game than a tennis match.

Our first trip to Oklahoma turned into an enormously moving experience. On Saturday we visited the memorial for the Murrah Building bombing victims. The tiny empty chairs, each one representing an innocent life snuffed out too soon, provide a horrifying, graphic reminder of what man does to his fellow man. The surrounding area is covered with countless notes and mementoes left there by relatives, loved ones and sympathetic strangers. Reading those messages becomes almost too much to bear. A huge statue of Jesus, his back turned away from the violence with the quote "Jesus wept" at its base, sums up the horror that occurred there on April 19, 1995.

This experience coupled with the 9/11 disaster still fresh in our minds helps to put tennis and all sports into the right perspective. We so often tend to place too much emphasis on winning at sports, even at the junior level. We need to remind ourselves sports are meant to be fun and winning or losing a tennis match pales in comparison to more traumatic life experiences. Howard Cosell dubbed sports "the toy department of human life"—an apt description that we (especially those in the media) often forget.

Getting back to the toy department, Andy and Pete won their singles matches so we only needed one more win to clinch. Patrick chose Mardy Fish, one of James's best friends on the tour, to play with James. With a string of five consecutive losses, the doubles point had proved a problem for the US in the past. James and Mardy managed to break that string with a four-set victory, thus clinching a win for the US.

As soon as one team clinches it's traditional for the winning team to circle the court carrying their flag. They pass the flag around so each player gets a chance to hold it. Because the doubles point proved the decider, James and Mardy were the first to parade. Tom and I could barely contain our pride as we watched them circle the arena, and I can't begin to imagine how James felt at that moment. Someone snapped a picture of him just after the winning point and I had it enlarged and framed. Of all the photos taken of James over his career, that remains my favorite—pure joy.

For the next round of Davis Cup in April, the US had to play Spain, again with the home-court advantage. With Sampras and Roddick on the team, two of the fastest servers in the game, we chose grass, the fastest surface. Spaniards are more used to a clay surface, which is much slower—another reason to choose grass.

Tom and I again took time off work to cheer for the US. This time we traveled to Houston Texas. Sampras, the grass court master with more wins on grass than any other player, took on Alex Corretja in the first match. We settled back to watch a sure victory for the US, but Corretja played the match of his life and beat Sampras in five sets. Andy won his match so at the end of the day the score stood at one point each. This made the doubles point crucial. Patrick chose Todd Martin and James to try to get the point for us. They played well together, handled the pressure, and by the end of the day the US needed only one more match to clinch the victory. Andy was scheduled to play Corretja but during the fifth set against Sampras he had injured his wrist and was unable to play. This proved a huge break for the Americans. Alberto Martín, Corretja's replacement, not comfortable on the fast grass surface, could not compete with Andy's powerful game and the US went through to the semifinals.

The next round took place in September, and here our home-court luck ran out. We had to play the French team, and knowing our players struggled with the clay surface, they chose Roland Garros Stadium, the home of the French Open. Sampras was not available for this match so Patrick gave Andy and James the singles responsibilities.

Tom and I wanted to go, but traveling to Paris for a long weekend seemed so extravagant—something we would never have considered before James embarked on his tennis career. We mulled it over for a while, but after seeing it through this far we felt we had to make the trip, especially since James would be in a singles spot. The last time we went to Paris had been a free trip to the French

Perseverance Pays Off

Open when James was still in middle school and when we had no thoughts of him ever actually playing on those courts. Still awed by our youngest son's progress, remembering this played a big part in our decision.

Andy played first against the French number-two player, Arnaud Clément. He struggled with the slow French clay and couldn't come up with a win. James then went on the court against Sébastien Grosjean. He also had his problems with the clay and only managed to win one set. We needed the doubles point to keep us in the competition. Patrick felt Todd Martin and James, who had played together successfully in Texas and had also won a tournament together in Cincinnati, would prove the strongest duo.

Their opponents, Fabrice Santoro and Michaël Llodra, had also enjoyed some success playing together. That match turned into one of the most entertaining and most exciting I have ever watched. It proved a seesaw battle, ending in a five-set win for the Americans. If James ran through a bad spell, Todd managed to pick him up. Then when Todd started having problems, James seemed to fire him up. Finally they both played with incredible energy, feeding off each other's enthusiasm. They came back from a 2-1 set deficit to win the last two sets by identical scores of 6-4, 6-4. After the match, I remarked to Todd that James got fired up in those last two sets. "James lives fired up," Todd observed.

The US still had a chance, but it was a steep hill to climb. They had to win both singles matches on the third day. We watched Andy's match with mixed feelings. Of course we wanted Andy to win, but that would mean the hopes of the team would rest squarely on James's shoulders. I couldn't help wondering how he would feel and how we would feel watching that match. Andy lost to Grosjean in four sets so James's final match against Clement was meaningless. Asked how he would have felt had Andy prevailed and he would have had to play under so much pressure, James said, almost wistfully, "I would have liked the chance."

Mix It Up, Make It Nice

I recall Tom and me sitting on the plane on our way back to the States that Sunday evening. Two down-to-earth people, we always thought twice about spending money on extravagances, especially on ourselves. At one point we looked at each other, the same thought in both our minds. I voiced what Tom was thinking. "Are we crazy to make a trip like this?" I asked. "Paris for a long weekend?" We grinned at each other like two impish kids. Considering what happened in the next two years, I wish we had made a lot more crazy trips.

Between Davis Cup matches James steadily improved his ranking. After his surprising run to the semifinals in Tokyo he ended the year with good showings in two Challenger events—runner-up in Houston and winner in Knoxville Tennessee. This brought his ranking up to 74, and reporters began speculating as to how high he could climb, some predicting top 10, which at this point seemed totally unrealistic to us.

James's first tournament in 2002 was in Auckland New Zealand, a warm-up for the Australian Open. My oldest brother Ed had immigrated to Auckland in the '80s. I hadn't seen him since he punctuated his initial trip from England with a stopover in New York. I saw this as a great opportunity to visit Ed, who had some serious health problems and whose doctors had warned him his heart would not hold out much longer. I would then go on to the Open, the only Slam I had never attended.

New Zealand lived up to and exceeded all Ed and his wife Vi had told me about it. I saw spectacular scenery, gorgeous beaches and magnificent wildlife. Vi took me "tramping" with some of her friends, through fields filled with sheep, to stunning, almost deserted coastlines. We ate potatoes, carrots and beans from their garden, and picked grapefruit, oranges and lemons from their trees. Ed snapped a photo of me digging up potatoes. "Did you ever think you'd be digging potatoes in January?" he asked. Even when James failed to qualify for the Auckland tournament, it didn't mar the trip. I resolved to come again next year, and bring Tom with me.

Perseverance Pays Off

After a glorious week I left for Melbourne where I found James had drawn one of the seeds, Alex Corretja, in the first round. I had little hope of staying long in Australia, but James eked out a four-set win and moved on to face unseeded Stefan Koubek in the next round. James seemed to be on cruise control, winning the first two sets at 6-4 and 6-2; but Koubek, with his reputation for incredible comebacks, fought back and won the next three sets. Of course we were disappointed, but we could see James's game was improving and we looked forward to what the rest of the year would bring.

James eased his disappointment somewhat by stopping again in Hawaii on his return. This time he won the Waikoloa Challenger event. He came into this tournament as the top seed, so after all his hard work in the past two years he appeared ready to put Challenger tournaments behind him.

Now James was in a position to qualify for most ATP tournaments, and he gained a lot more points in February with a run all the way to the finals in an indoor tournament in Memphis. The final match turned into a thriller, with Andy Roddick taking the third set at 7-5. In his next tournament, San Jose, James reached the quarterfinals. Just one year ago he had played the qualifying rounds for these two events and had lost both times in the first round. What a difference a year and a ton of hard work can make.

Excited about James's recent successes, Tom and I made the trip to Miami in March for the Masters event, variously known as "The Lipton," "The Nasdaq" and "The Sony-Ericsson." Our third trip to this tournament, we favored this one for two reasons. First, it gave us an opportunity to spend a few days in Tampa with the boys before play started. Thomas and James had recently moved into their first house and we wanted to see how they were situated. Second, jaded by the New England winter, we looked forward to some Florida sunshine where Tom could get a jump-start on his golf game.

The previous two years we had not stayed long in Miami. James lost in the first round of qualifying in 2000, and in the second round in 2001. Now his ranking was high enough to put qualifying matches behind him—a huge step forward. Our stay this year proved much longer. He won three rounds in the main draw before losing to Hewitt in the round of 16.

In April professional tennis begins its clay court season. American players typically practice on clay only at this time of the year so it has become their least favorite surface. James surprised us by reaching the quarterfinals in two tournaments, in Houston Texas, then in Rome Italy, but he could only muster one more win in the next three tournaments on that surface. In complete contrast to the slow clay, the next professional tournaments take place on the fastest surface, grass. There are several grass court warm-up tournaments, the majority in England in preparation for Wimbledon.

On a previous visit to England when Ed, Nin, Albert and I took Mom's ashes over (she lived from 1897 to 1997) to rest in her husband's grave, we became reacquainted with several cousins. Geoff, one of the cousins on my father's side, lived in Southsea on the south coast and had plenty of room for us to stay with him. Pauline, the widow of our cousin Colin, lived in Haddenham, a village so quaint and unspoiled it almost looks like a movie set—too good to be real. Thatched cottages, leafy lanes, an ancient church complete with duck pond and a graveyard with lopsided gravestones, some dating back to the 19th century, and the inevitable village pub—it has all the components of a typical English village. For a few days we stayed in her roomy house, becoming acquainted with her children—three boys and a girl. I became especially close to Janice, her daughter, who over the years has become like the daughter I never had.

In 2000, the first time James became eligible to play the qualifiers for Wimbledon, I urged Tom to make the trip. I so extolled the beauty of the English countryside, raved about the historical sights in London and assured Tom all my relatives were anxious to meet him, it was easy to convince him to go. He knew how much it meant to me, for even after 45 years in this country I still call England "home."

Geoff and Tom became instant friends, possibly because Tom is such a good listener and because Geoff, a veteran of World War II, had so many stories to tell. He kept us spellbound as he relived the first years of the war, when Britain's downfall seemed inevitable, several years before the US came to the rescue.

He told of how he and his younger brother John had volunteered immediately when Hitler threatened the mother country. John, only 17, had to lie about his age. He joined the RAF, had his plane shot down over France, and was listed as MIA. Eventually the French Resistance smuggled him back to England. With communication almost nil, his parents had no news of him until he knocked on the door and greeted his mother with a cheery "Hallo, Mum." John subsequently married a French girl and, now in his 80s, lives happily in France.

Geoff told us of the early days of the war, when they were issued sticks with nails in the end to use as weapons. He told how he had been temporarily blinded by an explosion, and with John still missing he lay in a hospital hoping to eventually regain his sight. We heard about the constant air raids over London when his parents and younger sister would crouch under the kitchen table waiting for the "all clear." Listening to these stories from the past almost made us forget we had come to watch a tennis tournament.

James lost in the first round of the singles qualifier, but with Kevin Kim as his partner they won two qualifier doubles matches to put them into the main draw. The last match turned into a nail-biter, with our team eking out a victory at 10-8 in the final set. (They don't play tiebreakers for the last set.) Even in June England can be cold, and they played this on a bitterly cold day. I have photos of us bundled up on the sidelines, hoods pulled up, looking frozen. I don't know if it was the cold or emotion, but I do remember I couldn't control the chattering of my teeth throughout a match that seemed as if it would never end.

Mix It Up, Make It Nice

To young players on the pro tour, winning that last round of a qualifier for an important tournament is huge. It means they get paid for the days before the tournament starts, as well as for two more days after they are out of the tournament.

That year, either we made the trip mainly to see the country and the relatives, or else we had little confidence in James coming through the qualifiers, because our flight home was for the day Wimbledon started. We briefly considered changing the flight, but decided the added expense didn't warrant it. Before we left, we walked around the Wimbledon grounds, admiring the green and purple motif, watching preparations for opening day and soaking up the unique atmosphere. We enjoyed watching the players warming up on the Aorangi practice courts and seeing how many we could recognize. In all my years in England, I had never attended this event so this was a rare treat.

The following year James again lost in the singles qualifier—a tough match in which he won the first set in a tiebreaker, lost the second, again in a tiebreaker and then lost the third at 6-3; but playing with Mark Merklein who is now his fitness trainer, they won the doubles qualifier. This time we stayed to watch them play. Unfortunately, they drew Don Johnson and Jared Palmer, the eventual winners, in the first round. They put up a good fight but couldn't come away with a win. To me it was thrilling to think my son was actually playing in this hallowed tournament in my native land.

James had moved up steadily in the rankings during the first months of 2002 so the third time we made the trip to England James found himself seeded in a Slam for the first time. Now the press began to take notice and seemed overjoyed to discover he was half English. Reporters descended on me for interviews, and a television station had me talk to them from a roof looking down on the courts. Gazing at all those tiny green rectangles, they asked me to describe my feelings. My youngest son playing in the world's most prestigious tennis tournament—a tournament I only dreamed of attending in my youth, but never realized that dream—how do you find words to describe that? Trying desperately not to look foolish in front of thousands of people on both sides of the Atlantic, I'm not sure what I said, and up to now I've never found the courage to watch the tape of that interview.

James won his first match easily and the press went wild. His next match developed into an epic struggle with Richard Krajicek (a former Wimbledon winner) in which James lost the first two sets, won the next two, and lost the fifth, 11 games to 9.

Despite this huge disappointment, Tom and I had a wonderful time again in England. Geoff arranged for us to make a trip to France. Many of the French people still realize the debt they owe to Britain and when they discovered Geoff was a veteran they gave him the red carpet treatment. We visited Normandy beach, lying peaceful now in the afternoon sun. Relics of Churchill's brilliant invention, which enabled the troops to land, still litter the beach, and little children play in an out of them. It was a tranquil, overcast day and I spent a long time there, gazing down at the beach, trying to imagine scenes of some 65 years ago.

Before leaving England, James and Brian came with us to Banbury, my hometown. We visited his grandmother's grave and I showed him the house where I grew up, and my school. We went onto the sports field where he saw the scenes of my track and field exploits. We had lunch in the pub across the street from my house. When we lived there, it had been a barrack for US soldiers—convenient for my sister who was dating age and who became very popular with the men stationed there. Albert and I had only to mention her name and the men showered us with gum, peanuts and candy bars.

Since the year 2000, James's first full year on the tour, I have visited England every year except 2004, our year of tragedy, the year James was injured and couldn't play. James's tennis career has brought me so many benefits. For this one, I am especially grateful.

Mix It Up, Make It Nice

The playing fields of Banbury.
James watches while I jump over Brian.

In August, James reached another milestone in his career when he won his first ATP title at the Legg-Mason tournament in Washington DC. Ironically, Brian, who had now been with him constantly for more than a year, had to miss this tournament for his sister's wedding. Evan Paushter, James's best friend since high school, stood in as his coach. Evan announced to all that James would win under his guidance, but with such players as Andre Agassi and Andy Roddick in the draw, that seemed a little optimistic.

Tom's best friend from the service, Ray Pitts, lives in Washington, and since it's driving distance we decided to go. Play began on Monday, but Tom, again reluctant to take too much time off work, declared we would drive down on Thursday.

"But he might lose before that," I said.

"He won't," he assured me, evidently as confident as Evan.

Not convinced, I rode the train, hoping I would still be there when Tom arrived so we could drive back together.

Perseverance Pays Off

As the sixth seed, James received a bye in the first round and didn't have to play until Wednesday. Tom left Fairfield on Thursday afternoon, arriving in time to see James notch a victory over Guillermo Coria. Next day James won a straight-set match over Alex Corretja. Now in the semifinals, James had to play Agassi, the top seed. This turned into one of those magical matches where James could do no wrong. Players call it "zoning." Every shot he hit landed right where he aimed it. He won the first set at 6-3, and we knew if he maintained that level of play he couldn't lose. Even so, at the changeover, needing only one more game for the match, James said that was the longest 90 seconds he ever experienced.

After such a huge victory, we thought James's confidence would carry over into the final match. His opponent, Paradorn Srichaphan from Thailand, had up to now never beaten James. We felt confident if James could play as he did the previous day there would be no contest.

With the temperature over 100 degrees, James and Paradorn battled for more than two hours. In contrast to his play the previous evening, James, at first, could do little against Paradorn's inspired play and he lost the first set at 6-1. He regrouped for the next set, which turned into a nail-biter. At 6-6 they played a tiebreaker that had us on the edge of our seats until James pulled it out at 7-5. In the third set James managed to break his opponent's serve once, and he ended with a 6-4 win.

The photographs of James hoisting the trophy reflect the joy he felt with this accomplishment. As soon as he won that last point he came over to where Tom and I sat in the front row and hugged and kissed us both. We could hardly believe our youngest son had come so far. In his early racket-throwing days, in those years when he struggled to achieve a New England ranking, in his high school years wearing a full-body cast every day, no one could have predicted this moment.

Apparently Brian had not expected James to reach this level of achievement either. Rashly, he had promised to skydive if James ever won an ATP event. Since then he has been more careful with any bets he makes.

Mix It Up, Make It Nice

After a week off it was time again for the US Open. We normally try not to look ahead in the draw, taking each match as it comes. Not so the media. They soon realized if James and Lleyton Hewitt both won their first two matches, they would play a reprise of their controversial match from last year. When this happened the press gave their upcoming meeting a huge build-up. What would be the demeanor of the players? What about the linesmen and other officials? Would they risk having an African American linesman? (They didn't.)

The match lived up to all expectations. James won the first set in a tiebreaker, dropped the next two but took the fourth set at 6-3. Then Hewitt proved he still had the edge by winning the deciding fifth set at 6-3. Both players showed great decorum throughout the match. Hewitt abandoned his trademark fist pumps and shouts of "C'mon." In fact a column in the *Daily News* by Lisa Olsen marveled at the way James's demeanor seemed to have rubbed off on Lleyton. At one point in the fifth set a spectator yelled, "Don't let him win, James. He's a racist." After the match ended, while shaking hands, James apologized for that over-exuberant fan.

After the excitement of the summer, the rest of the year seemed like an anticlimax. James played several indoor hard-court tournaments in Europe. Growing up in New England that should be his favorite surface but the best he could muster was a quarterfinal in Vienna.

In November he came back to Fairfield to spend Thanksgiving and Christmas in his hometown. We had a lot to be thankful for that year. We had no idea how short-lived our celebrations would be.

When sorrows come, they come not single spies
But in battalions.

—WILLIAM SHAKESPEARE

Chapter 10:
Tragedy

THE YEAR 2003 began well. Who would have believed it would end so badly? Invited once more to play in the Hopman Cup in Perth, James left early for Australia, always eager to represent his country. He had played this event once before, a few months after he turned pro. Except for a win over Wayne Ferreira (his first win over a well-known player), he had little success. This time, a more seasoned player and playing with Serena Williams, they won the trophy and each took home a platinum gold tennis ball with a map of Australia outlined in diamonds. Also notable was James's first success as a pro against Lleyton Hewitt. This meant nothing in the rankings, but it did a lot for his confidence.

Mix It Up, Make It Nice

I convinced Tom we should both go to the Australian Open in January. I had gone by myself in 2002, mainly to visit Ed, my oldest brother who lived in New Zealand and who had been in poor health for some time. The doctors feared his heart was growing weaker so I made the trip, thinking it might be my last chance to see him.

Ironically, Ed survived until 2006, while it was Tom, always bursting with health, whose days were numbered. This cloud hadn't yet descended and we spent a glorious week in New Zealand with Ed and his wife Vi. I went tramping again with Vi and her friends, through sheep-filled fields and along breathtakingly beautiful coastlines, largely unpeopled. Tom indulged in his favorite pastime—golf, with Vi's sons on spectacular courses.

From New Zealand we went to Sydney where James was playing in a warm-up event before the Open. A guide met us at the airport and escorted us to the tournament. James lost a close match to Carlos Moyá but we didn't let that spoil our vacation. Our guide Alex (arranged for us by a good friend in Connecticut whose son lives in Sydney) made sure we saw much of what Sydney has to offer. We went to the zoo, to Bondi beach, to the Opera House; he showed us the best places to dine and he introduced Tom and Brian to one of the most beautiful golf courses they had ever seen.

From Sydney we flew to Melbourne for the Australian Open, affectionately known as Oz. The weather was glorious; it seemed strange and wonderful to experience mid-summer in January. (My brother has said after more than 20 years "down under" it still didn't seem right to celebrate Christmas on the beach.) In James's first match against Jiří Vaněk he quickly lost the first four games but rallied to turn the set around and take it in a tiebreaker. Then he won the next two sets, 6-4, 6-4. Playing well, he won the next round against José Acasuso in three sets. He played his third round in the main stadium, Rod Laver Arena—his first time there—against Alberto Martin. James played well and won in four sets. It was the middle of the day and we sat in full sunlight. I watched the match swathed in towels with only my eyes exposed, for the weather had turned hot and we heard countless warnings about burn times because of the thin ozone layer in that part of the world.

Now we faced a dilemma. Not thinking he would still be playing in the second week ("Nice confidence, Mom!"), we had booked our flight home for that weekend. After much debate about the cost involved, we decided to change our flight and stay for the next match. Unfortunately James lost in four sets to Rainer Schüttler, who then went all the way to the finals before losing to Andre Agassi.

Despite the loss this had been a trip to remember and savor. We stayed in a hotel where many of the players were staying so each day the tournament provided transportation to the site; but most of the time Tom and I preferred to walk. The way led along the Yarra River and we enjoyed watching the skiffs gliding along the murky water, their coach biking alongside calling out orders on his megaphone. I showed Tom places I had discovered the year before; the second-hand book shop where you could buy a book, read it, then swap it for another; the mid-eastern take-out where the owner encouraged us to take as many falafel as we wanted and not to skimp on the tahini sauce; the souvenir shops along Flinders Street. Together we discovered new treasures. Vacations with Tom were so easy and stress-free. We always agreed on how and where we wanted to go, what and when we wanted to eat. After more than 25 years together, Tom and I still delighted in each other's company. We enjoyed simple pleasures and needed little to make us happy; and of course we gloried in our sons' successes. We would often marvel how our sons had turned what we had thought would be just a pastime into an exciting and fulfilling career that had added a whole new dimension, not only to our lives, but to others in the family as well as to many of our friends.

After making it to the round of 16 at Oz, James's hard work continued to pay off. In February he reached the semis in San Jose and the quarterfinals in Scottsdale and Indian Wells. Tom and I made two more trips to watch him play; Miami in March and Houston in April, where he didn't do as well, but it was always fun to go to these big tournaments, especially when we went together.

D URING THESE FIRST months of the year Tom visited the VA hospital in West Haven several times. I began to wonder about it.

"Why are you having so many checkups?" I asked him one day.

He laughed. "Don't you know I'm dying?" he asked.

I just laughed with him, for as long as I had known Tom he had enjoyed perfect health. He shrugged off sickness and never succumbed to it. In almost 30 years he had not missed a single day of work due to illness. Because of this I felt guilty if ever I got sick and couldn't just shake it off as he did.

I also noticed he didn't enjoy his food as much. He was eating less and though he could ill afford it he was losing weight. He tried to hide it from me and when I questioned him he made light of it. I suppose one reason I didn't worry too much was he still maintained his rigorous life-style of tennis, golf, weight-lifting and early morning calisthenics, with occasional bike-riding or jogging when he could fit it in—all while holding a full-time position with 3M. If he can do all that, I reasoned, he can't be too sick. Unfortunately I had not taken into account his indomitable will.

That was the end of that until I began making plans to go to England again in June. It had become an annual event for us because we had enjoyed it so much in the previous three years. After all the good times we had there, I assumed Tom would go with me again. We found so much more than tennis to keep us occupied. We would spend time again with my relatives and that "tight little island" always offers more sights to see.

Tom said since he had taken so much time off for Australia he couldn't afford to lose more time from work. I tried to persuade him, told him we should seize the moment, reminded him of the good times we had on our previous trips, but he remained adamant. My sister planned to go with me and he convinced me I should still go and enjoy being with her. Though I love my sister dearly, this prospect was not as attractive as spending the time there with Tom.

Tom waited until I had booked my ticket and arranged for us to stay with a cousin who lived close to Wimbledon before he mentioned another reason for not going. He told me he had to have a minor operation at the VA Hospital during that time.

"Why didn't you tell me that before?" I asked. "I'm staying home."

"You've already got your ticket," he said (I'm sure he delayed telling me on purpose). "Your sister's counting on you," he went on. "And anyway it's only a minor problem— I'll be home before you get back."

Still not convinced, I told him I didn't care about losing the money for the ticket. If he was in the hospital, I wanted to be with him.

He wouldn't hear of it, and—I'm sure my children will bear me out on this—when Tom told you to do something, you did it.

Reluctantly, I said good-bye to him, making him promise to e-mail or call to keep me informed. I couldn't rid myself of a nagging feeling this was not as minor as he would have me believe.

As soon as I arrived, I confided my fears to Brian, James's coach. Over the many years Brian has coached our sons, he and I have built up a very special relationship. I can always count on his sympathetic ear when I have problems. I told him I was worried about Tom, but wasn't sure if I needed to be. We both agreed we would say nothing to Thomas and James until they were out of the tournament. We knew for certain this is what Tom would have wanted. In fact, he wouldn't want us to tell them at all.

James won his first round, then two days later played an uninspired match and lost to Sargis Sargsian. The way

James played this match almost had me thinking he already knew about his dad, for his body language reflected the way I felt. At that point I had been away for almost a week with no word from Tom. My calls and e-mails went unanswered. I called Erika who told me Tom had come into the club with an armful of rackets he had strung and told her he couldn't string any more for a while. I didn't like the sound of that. Immediately, I called the airline and changed my flight to the next day. My sister did her best to talk me out of it.

"It's going to cost a lot extra."

"I don't care."

"We're supposed to visit the relatives."

"I don't care."

"It's probably nothing to worry about."

"I hope you're right, but I'm going anyway."

I spent the rest of the day packing and then walked to the house where Thomas and James were staying. I had to explain why I was cutting short my vacation. I can still see the frightened looks in their eyes at the thought something might be wrong with their dad. They sensed it must be serious to warrant my giving up time in my beloved England.

The next day became an endless nightmare. I left London in the afternoon and arrived seven hours later at Kennedy, where it was still afternoon. By the time I finished with customs and made my way to Connecticut, it was early evening. I opened the front door and shouted, "Anybody home?" Silence. My last forlorn hope gone, I looked up the number for the VA Hospital in West Haven, my hand shaking as I ran my fingers down the page. Still hoping the operation was minor; I asked when Tom could come home. The nurse's voice seemed to register disbelief at my ignorance as she told me he must stay for some time, but she offered nothing more. She did tell me although normal visiting hours end at 8 they would make an exception in this case. That made me worry even more.

Tragedy

I wanted to know why, but she was through giving out information.

I couldn't get to the hospital fast enough. My thoughts ran wild as I drove up I-95. I arrived as everyone was leaving. The hospital seemed woefully understaffed and I had trouble finding Tom. When I did find him, I could only gape in horror and disbelief. My tower of strength, my iron man, lay supine, tubes protruding everywhere from his lean body. Monitors beeped and something gurgled at the foot of the bed.

Dazed and fighting tears, I asked, "Tom, what happened?"

He managed a thin smile, looked ruefully at his spare body and said, "They really did a job on me, didn't they?"

I found out he had cancer. More widespread than the X-rays indicated, they had had to remove his entire stomach and part of his esophagus.

I sat with him until they forced me out at 11 p.m. Doped with morphine, Tom was barely lucid and often hallucinated. I was having trouble coming to grips with this. Many thoughts went through my mind as I kept my lonely vigil. I gazed at this man who has been my hero, the man who gave his sons their values to live by, who drummed into them the importance of education, who knew how to temper discipline with love, who taught them to play and love the game that brought us together and has meant so much to us and who had just begun to see amazing results from all he taught them. It wasn't fair.

Reluctantly, I kissed him good-bye and somehow found my way through the maze of eerily quiet corridors to the parking lot, and drove home. Zombie-like, I wandered aimlessly through the desolate house. I found myself in the basement, not knowing why. It was dark but I didn't bother to turn on a light. At other times with Tom away, I'm apprehensive of the dark, but then I could think of nothing but Tom. I didn't know what to do or what to think. I made my way upstairs and tried to sleep. Although I'd been awake for 24 hours, sleep didn't come. A warm, humid night, I tossed and turned, alone with my thoughts. At 3 a.m. the nightmare continued. The phone rang. Concerned about his father, James called from a stopover in Italy. I had to break the sad news about his father's illness. He was calling with the hope it wasn't as bad as he feared, and I had to dash that hope. How difficult it is to hurt someone you love. I was reminded of how my mom couldn't bring herself to tell us of my dad's unexpected, early death. Now I had a similar task.

After we cried a little together, I arranged to pick him up at Kennedy in the afternoon, wondering how I'd make it if I didn't get some sleep. Thomas was on a different plane. I still had to tell him—small wonder sleep eluded me.

Thomas, on a later plane, took the limo home. James broke the news to him. We were all fighting jet lag, but they wanted to visit their father right away, so we drove to the hospital. On the way, I tried to prepare them, but their faces still registered horror and disbelief at their first sight of him. We attempted to be upbeat, but Tom seemed to handle it better than we did.

The next day, the doctor arranged a family meeting at Tom's bedside. For this, Tom, ever the fighter, had made the effort to get out of bed and was sitting in a wheelchair. The doctor told us his disease is called linitis plastica, a particularly virulent cancer that attacked Tom's stomach and esophagus, but she blithely assured us he could live for one or two years. The way she said this seemed to imply this was good news, but it left us stunned—the first inkling we had the illness is terminal. At first frozen into silence, I recovered, grasped Tom's hands and looked deep into his lovely, tear-filled eyes.

"We'll fight it," I told him. "You've got so much to live for."

He put on a brave face and turned to his sons, also stunned into silence.

"Hey, you guys," he said, "I want a major before I go."

I'm sure tennis was far from their minds, but they both nodded numbly and said, "Sure, Dad."

Tragedy

While we were talking, Wimbledon continued on TV, then into the second week. How far off and unimportant it seemed.

I'll never forget leaving the hospital that day, the three of us walking through the desolate hallways, past the deserted coffee shop and the empty cafeteria, not talking, but feeling each others' pain. I'm trying to find the words to make them feel better while they each have a protective arm around me, tacitly assuring me they will always be there for me. We're all trying to hold back tears.

Tom stayed in the hospital for two weeks. During the first week, Thomas and James, at their father's insistence, played in a tournament in Newport Rhode Island, Thomas in the qualies, James in the main draw and together in the doubles. West Haven is on the way to Newport, so I developed a routine of driving to the hospital, spending several hours with Tom playing cards or Scrabble or just talking and then driving on to Newport where I spent the night. The next day, I watched whichever son was playing, then drove back, stopping for several hours at the hospital before driving home to my lonely house. I did this until they were out of the tournament, and all the activity helped me over a difficult time. During the second week, Tom began to get stronger, and he and I went for long walks around the hospital grounds. His room was on the third floor, and he insisted on walking up and down the stairs each time we went out. He was determined to fight this.

The boys continued their tennis careers. Tom remained upbeat and seemed convinced he would recover. We couldn't attend any of the matches then, but we watched them together whenever they were on TV. I particularly recall James playing the Cincinnati tournament in August. We were at the hospital for a check-up while James was playing his second round, and we saw him win it on the set in the waiting room. In the next round he played Andy Roddick. It happened to be the night of the massive blackout in the East, but by some miracle we still had power. While all around us the lights were out, we watched an amazing first set, which James lost in a tiebreaker. James was playing as well as we had ever seen him play. Unfortunately, he couldn't maintain that level in the next set. In the post-game interview James, as usual, was saying all the right things. Just as they took the microphone away, he pulled it back, looked right into the camera and said, "I love you, Dad." I immediately melted into tears, but Tom's reaction was the just the opposite. Enraged, he jumped to his feet and said, "He's got to think about his career. I don't want him worrying about me." The phone rang, interrupting his tirade. "I know who that is," I said. "It's Erika, and she's crying." It was Erika and she was crying. "That kid is some class act," she said through her tears. I agreed.

Not long after Tom had left the hospital, tragedy struck again. His mother, ailing for several years with diabetes and kidney failure, died on July 29. On the weekends before she died, although Tom was so ill, we drove down to his parents' home in Peekskill New York. We would take volumes of short stories to read to her, for the diabetes had taken its disastrous toll—she was blind and had had both legs amputated. We took turns reading to her and then discussing the stories we had read.

For the funeral Tom had to wear a suit, which greatly upset him for it emphasized how much weight he had lost. He was trying so hard to seem normal and didn't want to draw attention to himself. Luckily he had two strong sons and two younger brothers to do the pall-bearing duties. After the funeral, the four of us went out for a quiet lunch and tried to regroup again after this latest blow to our family.

When the US Open began in late August, Tom was beginning to get stronger but he still looked emaciated and unhealthy. He refused to go to James's first match because he knew the camera would be on the family box and he was trying not to let his condition be known. We persuaded him to go to the next match against Sargsian but he insisted on sitting in the back of the box. It turned out to be a great match, which James won in four close sets. Next up was Roger Federer, and although James played his heart out Roger prevailed. I know James was thinking of his father's request in the hospital, so the loss was doubly disappointing.

We decided to transfer Tom's treatment to Sloan-Kettering in New York. His doctor there urged him to do all he could to get stronger. He told us walking would help, so Tom and I went on ever more ambitious walks. At first I slowed down to keep pace with Tom, but soon he was going further and further, often up hills, and he had me panting to keep up with him. I was constantly amazed by his will to get better. Soon, he felt strong enough to resume work at 3M. His fellow workers tried to convince him he could go on disability but he wouldn't hear of it. Although most of his nourishment now came through a tube at night and although he now took dozens of prescription pills he wanted to act as if things were still normal.

His doctor told him of a new, experimental treatment for his cancer that involved chemotherapy. We talked it over, and Tom decided he wanted to try it. He had to stop in at Sloan several times each week for a blood stick, but he did it before work and didn't let it interfere with the rest of his day. When he went for the chemo I always went with him. It gave us a chance to talk with the doctors. I couldn't shake the feeling they weren't telling us all we needed to know, that Tom's case was hopeless and this new method would do no good, but I didn't know the right questions to ask, and neither did Tom.

After the Open, James went into a slump. He played four more tournaments but lost in the first round in three of them and won one round in the fourth. I don't know what was going through his head at this time, but I believe when he shaved his head on his birthday (December 28), it signaled for him a new beginning. He had a new look and I think a new determination to try to fulfill his father's hospital wish. What happened in the following year proved once again Robert Burns knew something when he talked about "best laid schemes" and how they "gang aft agley" (often go awry).

On the last day of the year Tom and I "celebrated" in a way that had now become something of a tradition. We sat by the fire and discussed the ups and downs of the year just past. In spite of what seemed a preponderance of downs, Tom managed to come up with a lot of positives. One of these was how thankful he was to be the one with cancer. "If one person in four gets cancer," he said, "I'm glad it wasn't you, or Thomas or James."

When midnight struck we toasted each other with sparkling apple cider and welcomed a New Year—our last one together.

When to the sessions of sweet silent thought
I summon up remembrance of things past,

—WILLIAM SHAKESPEARE

Chapter 11:
Memories

FAST FORWARD TO Norfolk Virginia in December 2006, where James held his second exhibition to benefit cancer research. He did this to honor his father's memory and it went so well he decided to make it an annual event. Another reason for holding it again was because Andre Agassi had agreed almost a year earlier to take part in it. The Bryans, twin brothers, contemporaries of James's and one of the top doubles teams in the world, helped out; as did Boyd Tinsley, trained as a classical violinist and a member of *The Dave Matthews Band*. With such celebrities volunteering their time, the event seemed certain to be a success.

Mix It Up, Make It Nice

Just after I arrived on Thursday morning they whisked us over to Old Dominion for a very well-attended luncheon. All, I'm sure, paid big bucks for the privilege of eating in the same room with some tennis greats. James, Andre, the Bryans—Bob, Mike and their father Wayne, and I, along with some people from Anthem Blue Cross (the sponsors) sat at the head table and the emcee selected questions for us from the audience. Most of the queries went to the players, but there must have been some tennis mothers in attendance for a few questions came to me. One asked about James's early days in tennis.

"He was a brat," I told them. "He had a huge temper which he often vented on an old racket which he carried in his bag just for this purpose."

I continued in this vein for a while, describing how inappropriately James handled his frustrations, and how much grief they caused his coach and us. When I seemed to be finished, James chimed in. "I was waiting for a 'but,'" he said.

Hastily, I pulled the microphone back toward me and added, "But he's turned into a really a good sport now." Laughter and much applause.

They also asked when we realized he would try to make tennis his career.

"Not until his second year in college," I told them. "Until then it was just a dream. Around age 10 he fantasized about playing tennis for a living, but later he felt he would have had a better chance of winning the lottery than becoming a professional tennis player."

Andre then related his completely opposite experience.

"At age 4 my father introduced me to everyone as the future number-one player in the world," he said. "And he did all he could to make it happen." Andre confessed he was not too happy when he first went to a tennis academy, but as long as he had to be there he might as well do his best. One of the very few who made it, I would be surprised if he doesn't bear some scars from that experience.

Memories

Wayne Bryan (the twins' father) then remarked on my composure when watching James play. (Wayne always says lovely things about me, some deserved, most not.) I told the audience I wasn't always so composed and James corroborated that.

"Brian Barker, James's coach," I told the audience, "not only teaches tennis. He also teaches parents how to behave. After I reacted quite violently to a missed overhead in a 12-and-under tournament, he told me I should try to conceal my feelings in case James looked up at that crucial moment." Observing James's reaction as I told this story, it seems he did look up at that crucial moment.

Since then, I've tried hard to keep my composure. It wasn't easy in junior matches because it took a while for James to accept losses gracefully, but now that he behaves himself on the court, it's a lot easier.

I have another reason for staying calm, especially at matches with TV coverage. I've noticed the cameras like to pick up on parents who get excited when watching their offspring, so I figure if I don't act up they might leave me alone. I would rather they focus on the court; James is much better looking.

At the event that evening I met an old friend, Geoff Grant. Geoff, an All-American from Duke University, played on the tour for eight years, becoming the tenth best player in the US in 1998. He graduated with a degree in political science, and now works for The Tennis Channel as an analyst for ATP tournaments.

Geoff was often in Boston when Thomas attended Harvard and would very graciously come to the Harvard courts to hit with Thomas, and a few years later with James. He helped their games enormously, and I think they were awed and gratified to hit with someone who actually had tour experience. At that point they had probably begun to entertain notions of trying the tour, and they enjoyed hearing of his experiences as well as hitting with him.

Geoff and I talked over old times while waiting for the exhibition to begin, and after listening to a couple of my

153

anecdotes, he told me I should write all this down. I agreed, and that's the reason for this chapter.

First, we talked about last year's exhibition and Geoff asked me about John Mayer, who donated his valuable time to perform in it. John also comes from Fairfield. After high school he studied at Berklee College of Music in Boston, and has become an extremely popular singer, songwriter and one of the most accomplished guitar players in the world. My story about how John's mother used to drop him at our house early in the morning with his two brothers, Carl and Ben, fascinated Geoff. Margaret, their mother, didn't want her boys walking to school in all weathers and her workday started early so she asked if they could wait at our house for the bus to the middle school that Carl, John and Thomas attended. Ben and James still went to grade school and since they went later I could drop them off on my way to work.

They had some free time before the bus came and one day John started playing with a keyboard, one of our boys' Christmas gifts. Thomas and James inherited little of their grandparents' musical talent and John was producing much better sounds from the keyboard than any I had heard from my boys. He asked if he could borrow it for a while. On the strength of that, I told Geoff, James claims at least partial credit for John's amazing career. Incidentally, I don't believe John ever returned the keyboard.

Somehow the subject of Grand Slams came up. I told Geoff I had seen James play in all of them except the French Open, but we did go to the French when James was 12 and Thomas 15. Thomas and I won a mixed doubles tournament sponsored by Orangina. The grand prize was a trip for four to the French Open. A family tournament, the teams had to be either mother/son or father/daughter. Any child with a national ranking could not enter, but this happened to be the year before Thomas, a late bloomer, appeared on the national list. Local and sectional play proved not too challenging but then we played the finals at the West Side Tennis Club. Here we had to play three matches and we managed to win them all. I particularly remember the semifinals against a strong father/daughter team. The daughter played on her college team and the father was no slouch. Thomas at 6'5" possessed a formidable serve but he refused to use it against the girl.

"Thomas, this is for a trip to Paris," I reminded him but he still couldn't bring himself to do it, although her father had no such qualms when serving to me. In spite of this we managed to win in three close sets. We took the final in two and we had our trip to France. What a glorious trip it was!

James, me, Thomas at the Louvre. Thomas and I won a trip to the French Open courtesy of Orangina.

We flew business class on Air France, something our sons had never experienced. They sat there in their glory, accepting the attention from the stewardesses as if it were their due. They had their own room at the Hotel Baltimore, which also pleased them immensely, especially when they discovered their TV provided all the cable channels. We spent two days at the French Open watching the likes of Pete Sampras, Stefan Edberg and MaliVai Washington. The rest of the time we explored Paris. Shunning the tourist buses we did our own walking tour, beginning at l'Arc de Triomphe, proceeding down the Champs-Élysées, taking in, among other well-known attractions, Les Invalides, the Louvre and the Left Bank. The tour ended at the Eiffel Tower, just a short walk from our hotel.

On another day we found some clay courts that looked very similar to the clay at Roland Garros. We played some family doubles, never dreaming several years hence James would actually play on the clay courts at the French Open, for at this point few people would have given James a chance at a career in tennis.

NOW THAT JAMES HAS become somewhat famous I've thought quite a bit about fame since it happens to so few and since it has unexpectedly happened to us. When James first began to make a name for himself, Selena Roberts, who now writes for *Sports Illustrated* but was then with *The New York Times*, interviewed me, asking me how it felt to have a famous son. I told her I had never been overly impressed by fame and I just hoped it wouldn't do anything to change James and I would try to make sure it didn't. (James often says it's his mother who keeps him humble.) I particularly like Emily Dickinson's take on the subject. She calls fame "a fickle food upon a shifting plate." John Milton goes a step further and dubs it, "that last infirmity of noble mind."

It seems almost everyone is looking for his little bit of fame. Witness the hordes of people who go to great lengths to try to get their faces on TV, often making total fools of themselves. After the US Open, scores of people tell me, "I saw you on TV," as if I've achieved some great accomplishment. After the 50th person tells me, I have to curb that tendency to wax just a little sardonic.

I find this fascination with TV exposure difficult to comprehend. Few of us are attractive enough to warrant it. Even harder to understand is the adulation we heap on celebrities—movie stars, singers, athletes, politicians, even people who have done nothing except inherit lots of money. The Declaration of Independence says we are all created equal, yet in this country the preoccupation with fame seems greater than in most other countries. I'm mystified by the awe in which some of these "famous" people are held. As Father Joe said—we're all just people.

James and I received an invitation to a garden party in Washington DC honoring Queen Elizabeth and Prince Philip. I must admit I was somewhat awed and surprised by the invitation. I showed it to several of my friends. "Oh, you have to go," they all said. Perhaps if James were going I would have, but mainly because I enjoy spending time with him. I mean no disrespect to the Queen when I say my desire to meet her is probably about as strong as hers is to meet me. As I said to Selena, I'm not impressed by fame.

While I'm on this subject of fame, I should analyze my motives for writing this book. Could it be I'm looking for my little taste of fame? I would like to think my motives are purer. People all over the world ask me about the way we raised our children, and have suggested I write a book on the subject. I always give most of the praise to Tom, and I would like this book to be a tribute to him. Another reason I write is because it helps to deal with not having him around any more. I feel by writing about him and the family, reliving all the good and bad times we experienced together, I'm keeping him alive.

In *Le Petit Prince*, Antoine de Saint-Exupéry observed it's sad to forget a friend—"C'est triste d'oublier un ami." Before becoming my husband, Tom was a friend, and writing about him and our children helps ensure I will never forget my dearest friend.

Another reason—if this book can prevent just a few parents from pressuring their children to succeed so they can vicariously reap the ensuing fame and fortune it will be worthwhile. Perhaps after reading this parents might also realize the value of spending time with their children instead of heaping material goods on them in an effort to make up for time not spent.

Before sending a child off to pursue fame and fortune at any type of sports camp, parents should try to honestly appraise their motives. Do you have your child's best interests at heart? Is this really what he wants to do? Does she want to give up all the joys of a normal childhood and enter at an early age the cutthroat world of competitive sports? Consider playing for your high school team as opposed to playing for yourself. Instead of cheering on your friends to victory, you're only hoping they lose so it will enhance your standing. What kinds of friends can you possibly have in such a situation? A child who leaves family, friends and hometown gives up a considerable portion of his young life to pursue a dream, and while I don't know the statistics, I would guess the vast majority of those dreams go unrealized. When it doesn't work out (which is likely), what do these deprived children have to fall back on? Ironically, because of the pressure their level of tennis often drops, so not only have you compromised their education and possibly messed up their lives, their tennis has deteriorated too.

I believe many of these parents are adversely influenced by unscrupulous coaches who tell them their little darlings could be the next Sampras, the next Evert. Blinded by dreams of fame and fortune, they consider the tennis academy and are willing to pay the unrealistic, exorbitant fees these coaches demand for private lessons. I've seen many of these children turn into selfish brats, with little or no consideration for the parents who finance them. Unless they do become the next Sampras or Evert (about a one-in-a-million shot), they will be hard-pressed to realize a normal, happy, successful life.

When James first went on tour, in those years when he lost so much more than he won, Brian was able to encourage him to continue by reminding him he could go back to Harvard and a normal life at any time. This enormously relieved the kind of pressure I'm sure those prodigies from tennis camps experience.

During my 15 years at a tennis club, I frequently witnessed parental pressure. One of the worst cases occurred when a father brought his three-year-old in for private lessons. He had heard Andre Agassi's father had him hitting tennis balls at the same tender age so he thought this was the formula for success. None of the other pros wanted any part of it so Ed asked me. After I convinced Dad that 15 minutes would be the limit of Ryan's concentration, I took them both onto the court. Dad sat on the bench while I attempted to teach Ryan, who I realized almost immediately had absolutely no interest in tennis. He gazed around at the other courts, and I constantly had to bring him back to the matter at hand.

"This won't work," I told the father, thinking he would end the lesson. Not a chance. He made Ryan stay there for the full 15 minutes. When we went back to the desk, Dad asked me what he should do.

"Take him out with you and just have fun playing ball with him," I advised. "Play catch with him, work on his eye-hand coordination, then if he seems to enjoy it, bring him back in a couple of years."

Apparently, the man had a hearing problem because he then asked, "So when can we have another lesson?"

I tried another lesson, which went no better than the first. Then Dad came up with a brilliant idea. "Maybe if Ryan sits on the bench and watches me hit the ball with you he will want to play." Now he's paying private-lesson prices to play pitty-pat tennis with me, from service line to service line, while Ryan casts nary a glance at us. He's still more interested in everything else going on around him. After that, I finally convinced the father he was wasting his money. I didn't follow up on it but I would guess unless the father's attitude changed drastically Ryan would never be a fan of tennis.

Mix It Up, Make It Nice

Memories

Thomas, James and I,
Yonkers, 1981.

James ran as soon
as he could walk.

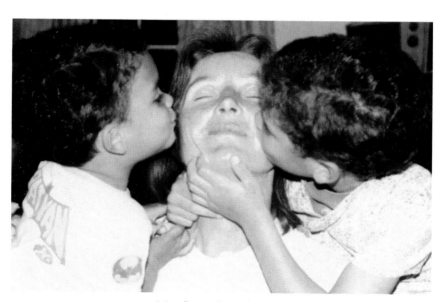

My favorite picture.

Mom and her four children. Ed, Albert, me, Mom, Nin.

James, me, Thomas and Gran, Yonkers.
Gran's 88th birthday party.

Memories

Thomas and James amusing themselves while we play.
Scalzi Park, Stamford CT.

Chris.

The family, circa *1988.*

Mix It Up, Make It Nice

James's high school graduation, 1997.

*Tom's mom, me, Thomas, James and Tom's dad
at their home in Peekskill NY.*

Memories

Tom with Brian Barker—more than a coach.

Tom and I at NCAAs, Athens Georgia, 1999.

My favorite picture of Tom. Love that smile!

Tom, Howard and I at the 2000 US Open.

Tom and Thomas, England 2001.
I like the love and pride in Tom's eyes.

With a kangaroo in Sydney, 2003.

*James and I outside my family house
in Banbury England, 2003.*

My new best friend.

Memories

Talking with Geoff about the days when Thomas and James were growing up triggered more memories.

I like to remind Brian of this episode whenever, courtesy of James, he is luxuriating in a five-star hotel in some exotic corner of the world. When James was about 12 and still very much a brat, Brian, Thomas and Mike Passarella, another tennis player in Thomas's age group, had planned a weekend in Newport Rhode Island to play golf and to watch Brian's friend Marc Kaplan play in the Hall of Fame grass court tournament. James, always wanting to do what his big brother did, pleaded to go with them but no one wanted him. Knowing how he would act up all weekend if he stayed home, I appealed to Brian. Grudgingly, he agreed to take James—not a popular decision with the rest of the group.

They had booked one room in a modest motel and had no intention of changing their plans to accommodate James. Brian and Mike had a bed each, Thomas had a cot and they gave James a pillow and blanket and put him in the closet. At the time he had to sleep in a full-body back brace to correct scoliosis. When he emerged from the closet in the morning, back brace over a singlet shirt, spindly legs sticking out from boxer shorts, Mike, as soon as he stopped laughing, commented, "This is one of New England's finest athletes?"

James got very little sleep, played golf badly and dozed off in the stands at the tournament, but he didn't want to miss that weekend.

Another lovely story about James began when he was only 6 or 7 years old. We had just moved to Connecticut and Tom was furnishing his office. Over his desk he hung a poster of a BMW sports car. Putting one arm around each child, he pointed to the poster and said. "You see that car? When you make your first million you can buy me one of those."

We all laughed and that was the end of it—or so I thought. In 2002, the first year I went to the Australian

169

Mix It Up, Make It Nice

Open, James told me if all went well that year he would be able to get Dad that car for Christmas. That was in January and I had to keep it to myself for the rest of the year. Things did go well and Tom got his sports car at the end of the year.

My gift from James that year was a calendar. Dutifully, I said thank you and commented on what a lovely calendar it was. (I must admit to a brief thought about Tom getting a car and me a calendar—but it was just a passing thought.) Photos of current tennis stars appeared on each month so I assumed James's picture must be on one of them. I flipped through the pages looking for him. "Keep going," James urged. Before I found his picture (July) I noticed a whole week in June had been highlighted. "That's the week you and Erika will spend at the Cape." He had reserved the cottage where we had always spent our family vacations until national tennis tournaments intervened. We hadn't been back to Cape Cod for years, but it remains one of my favorite spots in the world, and was one of the most thoughtful gifts I could have received. The cottage accommodates more than two people, so we invited two more friends and all had a vacation to remember.

Although Tom believed in disciplining our boys there was never any doubt about how much he cared for them. He insisted on respect for all people and they learned that lesson well. They often teased us both but we were all so secure in our love and respect for each other we were able to laugh at ourselves with them. One day Tom reminded Thomas he owed him a dollar. Thomas, who liked to flaunt the fact he was the tallest member of the family, and who at 6'5" towered over Tom, took a dollar bill out of his pocket, held it up as high as he could and said, "Dad, if you can reach it, you can have it." We all laughed—and Thomas kept his dollar.

We all teased Tom about how he always listened to other people's stories, but rarely talked about himself. I thought this was one of his more endearing qualities and is one few people possess today. Today, with most people it's "all about me." At one of the college tournaments Tom conversed at length with someone he had never met before, asking questions, hearing his life story.

Later this person discovered Tom was James's father, and James, the top seed in the tournament, had reached the finals. Tom's new friend went back to him and said, "How come you never mentioned James is your son?"

"You never asked," Tom replied.

Although I don't think our sons resemble each other too closely apparently others do, which has accounted for some amusing situations. One day at the local golf course, James handed the girl behind the counter his credit card to pay for his group. Thomas stood behind James and the girl kept looking his way and smiling. James brought her back to the business at hand and she apologized to him. "I'm sorry," she said, "But I think that might be James Blake standing behind you."

Another time James and Thomas were playing doubles at the Newport tournament. James prepared to serve and Thomas stood at the net. "Come on, James," I said, I thought under my breath. The man in front of me turned around and told me James was at the net and Thomas was serving. "No," I told him. "That's Thomas at the net." At this point the man became excited. He turned around to emphasize his point. "You don't understand," he insisted. "I'm from Fairfield—I know these guys. Thomas is serving." I was about to suggest a small wager with him when my sister spoiled everything by saying, "She should know—she's their mother."

JAMES AND ANDRE finished their match. The crowd loved it. Both said complimentary things about each other afterwards. The commentator asked Andre why he consented to play this exhibition. "Because James asked me," came the simple reply. The next day James returned the favor by participating in Andre's charity event in Richmond.

Mix It Up, Make It Nice

Thou'lt come no more.
Never, never, never, never, never.

—WILLIAM SHAKESPEARE

Chapter 12:
More Tragedy

EVEN WITH THE cloud of Tom's illness hanging over us, we kept hoping the New Year would bring an improvement. Tom stayed optimistic about his treatments from Sloan-Kettering, and he knew James, with his drastic new hairstyle, had a renewed commitment to his tennis career. We looked forward to seeing the results.

We didn't have long to wait. Selected again for the Hopman Cup, this time playing with Lindsay Davenport, they both played well and once again won the cup for the US. Full of confidence, he moved on to Melbourne and the Australian Open, the first slam of the year.

Mix It Up, Make It Nice

Because of Tom's condition we couldn't even consider making the trip "down under" this year, but together we watched the matches on TV. We watched James's first match with special interest. For Christmas, Tom and I had tried to think of something meaningful to give our sons. It's difficult to shop for someone whose paycheck is substantially higher than either of ours. We visited several jewelry stores and finally settled on a platinum-gold wrist chain for James and a gold neck chain for Thomas. At his post-match interview, Tom and I without mentioning it to each other noticed the chain on his left wrist at the same time. We turned to each other, our faces beaming. "He's wearing it," we said in unison. When we gave it to him we weren't sure if he would like it. Apparently we had no cause for concern—his father's last tangible gift to him, that chain has become one of James's most prized possessions.

That last paragraph leads to an illustration of how much "in sync" Tom and I were. One day a very young James came to me with a puzzled look on his face. "Do you and Dad talk to each other a lot?" he said. "Because when I ask him something, then ask you the same thing, I always get the same answer." I laughed and suggested, "Maybe it's the right answer." Another time Tom and I had a minor disagreement with Thomas. Tom and I held the same view while Thomas's was different. Frustrated and unable to make his point against our united front, Thomas put his hands to his head and groaned, "My God, where do I get my intelligence?" I laughed so hard that Tom, who was trying to look stern, broke down and joined in.

What might seem disrespectful to others is not viewed that way by us. Amongst the four of us there has always been a lot of good-natured teasing. Our boys know exactly where to draw the line, and they never step over it.

Towards my tennis game and me they are merciless. "Mom, if you didn't have luck, you wouldn't have a game," James has told me. Or "Mom, why do you bother to get your racket strung, you use the frame most of the time?" A classic line came from Thomas when he was coming off a court on which I was about to conduct a peewee clinic.

"You're going to teach?" he asked. "But what will they learn?" One of my (childless) friends overhearing this asked me, "Do you let them talk to you like that?" I assured her they meant no harm, and I was so secure in their love and respect for me I enjoyed their teasing. In fact I often retaliated, as when James, trying to belittle my track prowess, offered that "English athlete" provided a good example of an oxymoron. "Sort of like 'American literature'?" I shot back. "How come you guys are so good-looking?" I once asked James after yet another photo shoot. With a sidelong grin, he said, "It's a mystery, Mom, just like where we get our brains and our athletic ability."

As the first major tournament of the year, the Australian Open often produces unexpected results. Most players suffer from the time off over the holidays and we find out who has managed to stay in condition for the rigors of five-set matches in the broiling sun. James had prepared well and I believe he felt he had a good chance to go far. I know he wanted so badly to do this for his father, and with time running out, he probably felt this might be his best chance. Playing with confidence and determination, he won his first three rounds with the loss of only one set. In the round of 16 he drew Marat Safin. Safin is known as an enigma in the tennis world. Capable of breathtakingly brilliant play, he can also play well below his potential. Throughout this tournament he stayed on top of his game. James lost a close four-set match, which featured two tiebreakers. After that Marat went all the way to the finals, losing only to Roger Federer. James had come so close.

In February the US played the first round of Davis Cup competition. We were delighted when we heard it would be played in Connecticut, about an hour's drive from Fairfield. We felt sure the venue would clinch James's selection to the team, and it would mean Tom could watch him play again, for he could still travel short distances. I'm sure Captain Patrick McEnroe had no idea of the severity of Tom's illness (Tom effectively hid it from all of us) or he would surely have named James to the team. It was a bitter disappointment to us and to James, not only because he wanted his father to watch him play but also because he dearly loves to play for his country.

After this, James went into a slump. He had only four wins in his next three tournaments, twice coming up against an extremely talented but injury-prone youngster named Joachim Johansson. At Indian Wells he began to regain his form, making it to the quarterfinals. At this point, though, Tom and I had something else to think about.

During the first part of the year Tom struggled to maintain his work schedule. His sales group was in line to win the grand prize of a weeklong trip to Maui in March, and Tom fixed all his attention on that. As soon as we found out his team had won he started making arrangements. In his state of health this was obviously a trip he shouldn't make but he was determined to go. I think he realized this would be our last trip together and he wanted to make it memorable. Looking back, I know he made the effort more for me than for himself.

Tom wanted to give everyone on the trip a memento, so he came up with the idea of buying shirts for all his co-workers and their partners. We went shopping and selected a Hawaiian-style shirt for the men and a turquoise, v-necked shirt for the ladies. He ordered enough for everyone and then had each shirt embroidered with the person's name and "Maui, 2004." Then he packed them all in his bag, along with his clothes. His bag was ready to go a good two weeks before our departure date. We have made many trips together, but I've never seen him look forward to one as much as he did this.

He had other arrangements to make. To keep up his strength and try to gain back some of his lost weight, besides eating whatever he could during the day he ingested a food supplement throughout the night. He had to mail a week's supply of this to the hotel where we would be staying; making sure it would arrive before we did.

The plane trip proved difficult for him though he seemed reluctant to admit it. When we finally reached our hotel room he was totally spent. He took to his bed and had to spend all of the following day recuperating. He rigged up a makeshift IV system using a coat hanger and the bedside lamp so he could continue with his food supplement. I spent most of that day in the room with him, only leaving to find out what kind of food the corner store offered.

After a day's rest he felt much better and we set out to explore Maui. I found the tennis courts and two ladies who offered to play singles with me. Tom would watch us play, then take some photos when we finished. He didn't seem at all resentful that this game, which had played such an important role in our lives, was now denied him. He put on his happy face so I wouldn't feel guilty about playing when he couldn't. He did manage to play 18 holes on the beautiful golf course we had seen from our terrace. His co-workers couldn't believe the stamina he showed— that indomitable will again.

During the week we attended various dinners provided by his company. At one of these he presented the shirts and made a little speech thanking everyone for helping him through some difficult times. Everyone realized the significance of his gift and we all, even the men, had difficulty holding back tears.

One glorious, sunlit day we walked down to the beach. We found a place to sit on the rocks and together we watched huge waves breaking on the shore. Tom knows how much I love the ocean and he persuaded me to go in. I left him on the rocks while I walked down to the water's edge. I let the waves wash over me for a while, enjoying the feeling of calm they always bring, forgetting temporarily the dark cloud hanging over all of us. As I made my way back to Tom's place in the sun he snapped photos of me. He had a huge smile on his face, so happy to see me having a good time. I believe he enjoyed others' happiness as much, if not more, than his own. That's what true love is all about. In our current me-centered society we seem to have almost abandoned that particular form of happiness.

*Maui, March 2004. We're both wearing the shirts
Tom bought for everyone.*

The plane ride home again took its toll and he needed another day to recuperate, but I know he felt happy we had made the trip. I had tried to talk him out of it but he had set his mind on going. When he decided to do something he tried to let nothing get in his way. That's why his illness hit him so hard. He did everything he could to get the better of it and he always remained optimistic, but I believe he knew in his heart he was losing the battle.

After the Maui trip Tom still tried to keep up his work schedule. In fact he was at work on that May morning when I received a phone call from Italy. It's strange how you always remember where you were when you receive momentous news. I was ironing when the phone rang. Luckily James delayed calling until he could break the news to me himself. If someone else had told me he had broken his neck I would have imagined all kinds of horrors. On the phone he sounded fine. I'm sure this took great effort on his part but he didn't want me to worry too much. He spared me the details of the accident—I found out the whole story much later—and said he was coming home the next day and could we meet him at the airport. I abandoned the ironing and sat down to try to collect my thoughts. I felt like a fighter being punched when he's already down. How do I tell Tom and how will we handle this latest setback in our lives?

I couldn't provide details for Tom because I only knew what James had told me, but I assured him we would soon see for ourselves. Tom still insisted on doing the driving (no one in the family appreciates the way I drive) and we arrived just as the plane landed. James, his neck encased in a heavy brace, came through the door first with Brian hovering alongside like a mother hen. Laboriously, James walked towards us, trying his best to look normal. He hadn't seen his father since January and I know he saw the effects of his illness, but he hid his emotions behind a brave smile. Like father, like son; both tried to make the most of a bad situation, and seemed more concerned for each other than for their own plight.

We helped James into the front seat next to Tom, who still insisted on driving. Brian and I sat in the back. Although we didn't know it at the time, Tom would only be with us for two more months. We had no idea how serious his illness had become. James looked straight ahead, unable to move his head an inch from side to side, not knowing if he would ever play tennis again, yet the four of us bantered back and forth as if nothing were amiss. We discussed books. Tom and I always liked to hear about their current reading material. James had asked some of the other players about their reading habits and was surprised to discover few have done much reading, and even with all their travel time, they do little to change that. Reading had become a way of life for our children—wherever they go, they always carry a book with them.

Somehow the conversation came 'round to money. I often teased James about his expensive taste in clothing. "You pay so much extra just to have a fancy label sewn in the back of a shirt," I said, "And it's probably no different than one from Penney's." Then I moved on to precious stones. "Who can tell the difference between rhinestones and diamonds?" I asked. "When I go for a walk at night, the streets sparkle as brilliantly as any precious stones." The next day my words came back at me when James handed me a small box. "Happy Mother's Day," he said, "And they're not rhinestones." I've worn those diamond earrings ever since, but I would be wearing them had they been rhinestones or colored glass.

James has said breaking his neck was providential—one of the best things that happened to him, for soon after he returned to the States Tom's health began to decline rapidly. He could no longer work and didn't go far from the house. James, forced into temporary inactivity, spent a lot of time with his father. Had James been healthy, Tom would have insisted he play the Slams in Europe. James still treasures that time with his father, and looks on that injury as a blessing. After four years I still haven't been able to discuss those last weeks with James. I'm sure he obtained more valuable lessons from his father and came away with a different outlook on life. Someday I'll trust myself to talk about it with him.

With Thomas away most of the time still pursuing his tennis career (as Tom insisted he should), my youngest son proved a great comfort to me. We helped each other to shoulder our sadness. One day feeling lower than usual I asked him to go for a walk with me. We talked over the situation and he told me of his resolve to get better as quickly as possible because he knew how much we liked to watch him play. He didn't voice it but I'm sure he was also thinking of his father's hospital request. He felt time was running out. I had tried to tell him Dad didn't realize what he was saying; it was a spur-of-the-moment request brought on by the doctor's bad news. How difficult must it be to think clearly just after a doctor tells you your days are numbered? Normally his father would be the last one to put that kind of pressure on him. In an interview not long after Tom's death he shared a little of their conversations in his last days. "He didn't tell me to go out and win Wimbledon." Even so, I'm sure that first request stayed with James.

Now Tom took to his bed more and more. Realizing his time was getting short I tried to be with him as much as possible. He acquired a taste for tea, which he had rarely drunk before. He probably did it as a companionable gesture towards me with a nod to my English background, knowing how I still enjoyed a tea break. "Let's have a cup of tea," he would say several times each day. I would bring two mugs upstairs, then we would talk, mostly good memories or sometimes I would read to him. I think he enjoyed the warm feeling of sharing more than the tea, for his cup was often half full when I took it away.

When James came over, usually around lunchtime, I would leave for a while to run errands. Tom never insisted I be there all the time. In fact, he encouraged me to keep my part-time job at the tennis club and even to stay and play after work if I wanted to. If I did, I would always warn my opponent before we started I could only stay for one set. I never wanted to leave him for too long. Whenever I was out I always had the feeling in the back of my mind I had to hurry home again. After he died it was difficult for me to get used to having no reason to go home.

Those last two months have become a blur in my memory. I don't think any of us realized how little time we had left with Tom, and when we did we tried to deny it. It seemed we went from one crisis to another with Tom checking in and out of Sloan-Kettering for various procedures. I didn't know whether they were supposed to make him better or merely ease his pain. When he was in the hospital I visited him as much as possible. Sometimes Thomas or James would drive me there, but the traffic was usually so bad I found it just as easy to take the train. From Grand Central I took the subway as far as I could and then walked several blocks to Sloan. By the time I came home darkness had fallen. I always had a book but most of the time I gazed out the train window into the darkness and just let the tears flow.

Often in a rush to catch the earliest train I would find myself breathlessly running up the steps to the platform. This probably accounted for a vivid dream; so vivid I still remember it almost five years later. I'm running up a steep hill, constantly looking over my shoulder, trying to stay ahead of an enormous wave that threatens to engulf me. I didn't need a shrink to interpret that one for me.

Several times when Tom was home a crisis arose and we had to hurry him to the hospital. At these times it was a real comfort to have James or Thomas there. One Saturday in June James drove us to Sloan and let us out at the side entrance while he parked the car. After he drove away we realized the entrance was closed and we would have to walk around to the front. I took Tom's arm to walk around with him but he sank down on a wooden bench and forlornly looked up at me, "I can't, Bet," he said. I realized then just how weak he had become. Fortunately it was a fine day. I left him on the bench, raced around to the front door for a wheelchair and had him in the hospital before James returned. While Tom met with the doctors James and I looked helplessly at each other, knowing the worst but hesitating to ask his doctors.

During his last weeks we had an oxygen machine in the house. Tom could never be off it for long. Even on the rare occasions he came downstairs, he trailed a long cord behind him connected to the machine. When he went out, which was seldom, he trundled an oxygen tank along. One June afternoon we all went to a 40th birthday party of a very good friend, Rome, a tennis pro from our club. Physically extremely weak, Tom's mind stayed sharp. He sat watching a chess game when Rome, who was losing badly, had to leave for some birthday photos. Tom assumed his seat, finished the game and won it. Afterwards I told our friend, "You know, you won that chess game." Rome's jaw dropped. "That's humbling," he said. Just after that, panic struck when Tom's oxygen supply became alarmingly low. James and I hurried him into the car, getting him home just in time to hook him up to his machine.

Towards the end Tom must have been in serious pain but he tried to hide it from us. Although he always tried to be fiercely independent he began to realize his limitations. He told me I needed to learn how to replenish his food supplement. He also showed me how to administer an injection, a daily occurrence. I managed to do it right but it was difficult to find where to put it on his spare frame. He took in nourishment day and night yet he continued to lose weight. He spared me having to do these chores as much as possible for he knew I felt uncomfortable with them. Almost to the end he managed to take care of himself.

Increasingly uncomfortable, Tom went back to Sloan again. They performed an excruciating procedure to remove fluid from his lungs. I went with him and waited outside his room. When I saw him I could tell it had been a dreadful ordeal and I had difficulty stemming the tears. How painful it is to watch the suffering of someone you love. You want to bear the pain yourself. He endured it all for no reason for the relief proved short-lived. He came home again but after a few days could bear it no longer. One night he kept walking from room to room trying to get comfortable. Finally he told me to take him to Bridgeport Hospital. I stayed most of the night with him and then went back early the next morning. They put him in a temporary room, awaiting a hospice bed.

Now we knew the end was imminent but we didn't know how long. James sat in the room with me whenever he could. While his father slept, he told me I never had to be alone. "Wherever I go in the world, Mom, you're welcome to go with me," he assured me.

On the ride home that night I thought about St. Augustine. Somewhere in his *Confessions* he talks about the unbearable pain he feels when a dear friend dies and wonders if it's better not to become so close to anyone. Is it "better to have loved and lost than never to have loved at all?" I don't know the answer to that. Tom and I enjoyed 30 gloriously happy years together but now the thought of losing him seems too hard to bear. I can't imagine life without him. You have to take risks for happiness, a Jesuit priest once told me. Given life's transience any human relationship involves risk. Is it worth it? At this point, I wonder. I ponder a line of poetry: "One crowded hour of glorious life / Is worth an age without a name." Tom and I didn't need a "glorious life." We were both content to live "an age without a name" as long as we lived it together. When two people enjoy each other's company as much as we did, even the humdrum becomes joyful.

Knowing Tom would never come home again I tried to make his last days upbeat. I stayed with him each day as long as I could. When I left I told him we both had homework to do. We had to think of memories to talk about when I came the next day. Thirty years produce a lot of memories and together we lived again the good times and the bad—the vacations we had taken together: Cape Cod, Acapulco, Florida, England, Paris, Australia and of course Maui. We recalled the tournaments we had won together and moved on to our boys' tournaments, recalling how at first they lost many more times than they won. How important those losses seemed at the time, and how trivial they seem now. We went through the Harvard years, remembering the pride we felt when they received those acceptance letters. We lived again the years in Yonkers, our first house, teaching the boys to play tennis, reading bedtime stories.

Three days later James got to the hospital ahead of me. As soon as he arrived Tom urged him, "Get your mother here." James called me and I couldn't get to the hospital fast enough. His voice told me something was terribly wrong and I dreaded being too late. Every traffic light seemed an eternity. When I arrived Tom was barely lucid. He lapsed in and out of consciousness. Frantic, in one of his waking moments I held him, looked deep into his eyes and said, "Tom, my hero, you know who I am, don't you?" The memory of what he said next will go with me to my grave. He gazed at me with those lovely eyes while his lips formed the words, "My love."

James and I kept vigil all day until James had to leave to meet Thomas and go to Newport as his father had commanded. I resolved to stay the night at the hospital so before he left James went home to get me a toothbrush and a change of clothes. After he left the room became eerily quiet. The nurses brought me a reclining chair to sleep in but after several attempts to get comfortable I gave up and slid into bed beside Tom. He was so thin there was plenty of room and I enjoyed holding his hand

and feeling his warmth. The Mets were playing the Yankees and beating them. How we would both have enjoyed that in normal times. Now it seemed so unimportant—just background noise to alleviate the stillness.

Towards morning a nurse came in and checked on Tom. Then she left and sent in a grief counselor. I tried to listen but all my thoughts were with Tom. Nothing she said could have helped. The nurse came in again and told me it wouldn't be long now. Through my tears I asked her if she would stay with me. I had never been present at a death. I held Tom's hand and on the other side of the bed she monitored his breathing. At about 6 a.m. he drew his last breath. Still holding his hand I gazed for a while at his peaceful face, then through tears I looked out the window. The sky glowed red as the sun rose on a perfect summer day, and I knew whatever joys the future might hold, for me no day would ever again be perfect.

Mix It Up, Make It Nice

But O for the touch of a vanished hand,
And the sound of a voice that is still!

—ALFRED, LORD TENNYSON

Chapter 13:
Coping with Grief

WHAT DO YOU DO when you have just watched the person you love above all others take his last breath? How do you face life without the one who has been the main part of it for more than 30 years? I felt hopelessly lost and abandoned. Still holding Tom's hand, through tears I gazed, unseeing, out of the window, trying to collect my thoughts. A quotation came into my head from the past, from Nehru's eulogy for Gandhi—"... the light has gone out of our lives and there is darkness everywhere." That summed up my feelings. I felt as if I would be groping in darkness for the rest of my life, with no real direction.

Mix It Up, Make It Nice

Without Tom everything seemed meaningless. I used to tell him because of the discrepancy in our ages (I'm 10 years older) and given women live longer than men we would leave this world together. I had a vision of us walking hand-in-hand into the sunset of our lives, sort of like Deborah Kerr and Robert Taylor going joyfully to meet their Maker at the end of *Quo Vadis*. Yet considering Tom's glowing health and the pains he took to maintain it, I felt I would be hard-pressed to fulfill my end of the plan. Again I had to give the nod to Burns who seemed to know a lot about "best-laid schemes."

Finally I began to realize how selfish my feelings were. I was not the only one who suffered from this terrible loss. I had to let Thomas and James know. I called their cell phones. Both were turned off for the night so I left messages. Thomas had to play a qualifying match that day so it made sense to turn his off. James told me later he had left his on, waiting for the latest news of his dad, until a very late crank call made him turn it off. I remember the message I left for Thomas. "Your father died at 6:00 this morning. This is what I want you to do. I want you to go out and play your match for him today. That was what he wanted." I couldn't be there to watch but James told me later how proud he was of his brother that day. He played an inspired match and won it in a third-set tiebreaker. Dad would have loved it.

After delivering my heartbreaking news I wearily got up from the bedside, my limbs feeling like lead, picked up Tom's meager belongings and made my way out of the hospital. I drifted aimlessly through deserted hospital corridors, feeling as if I no longer had a place in this world, not knowing if I wanted a place in this world. At that hour of the morning few people stirred. Later I realized this was the middle of the July 4 weekend, which must have added to the early-morning quiet. I'm sure the nurse had told me what I needed to do but in my dazed condition it didn't register. It seems for all the other deaths in my family someone else had taken care of the details. Now it was up to me. I do remember going into an office to make a report but after that it's all a blur. I must have driven home and I must have called Tom's father, because he drove over from Peekskill and spent most of that day with me.

Before Pop arrived I went through the backpack Tom had hastily thrown together on that night I drove him to Bridgeport Hospital for the last time. I found a Harvard cap and two t-shirts—one said "Harvard Tennis" and the other was a New England shirt with a likeness of James on it. His last thoughts were of his sons and the pride he felt in their academic and tennis achievements. Then I found several sheets of writing. In his last days Tom had written to his two sons telling them how "proud, proud, proud" he was of them. First he talked of Harvard and their acceptance letters, then about their first contract with IMG and Nike. I showed them to Tom's dad and two days later gave them to Thomas when I went to Newport. He made a copy for James, and I still treasure my copy.

I called my sister. She had planned to visit for the Newport tournament. When I told her Tom had died she wanted to know if she should change her plans. I asked her to come. It would postpone for a little while my being alone in the house.

The next day we drove to Newport and watched James win his first match against Dick Norman. Thomas sat watching in the stands, too. The only overt acknowledgment of the monumental tragedy in their lives was the black wristbands they wore. Just as Tom didn't want to make a fuss when he first became ill, they knew he wouldn't have wanted his death turned into a media circus.

This was James's first match since his neck injury. I know he only played because his father had commanded it. Still not totally recovered from the effects of his injury, he admitted later it was the most difficult match he ever played. Although not enthusiastic about playing, it seemed evident he was determined to win—to win one for his dad. The first set turned into a squeaker—9-7 in a tiebreaker with James fighting for every point, but the second was a little easier and he won it at 6-3. As he shook hands after the match, he sought me in the crowd and gave a rueful smile. Sadly, I smiled back. How unimportant it all seemed to us at this point. Tom would not have appreciated this attitude, but the wound of his death was still so raw it was the best we could do.

James had proved his point, done what his father wanted, and he didn't seem to mind when he lost in the next round to Alex Bogomolov. It turned out James had strained a muscle in his arm by coming back too soon after a period of inactivity. This meant he and Thomas also had to pull out of the doubles after winning their first round. I think they felt they had more important things to attend to so they weren't too upset about it.

When I think back to those days after Tom's death, they all seem to run together. The vast numbers of cards and letters I received in the mail amazed me. People left flowers and food on my porch. Each time I came home I would find 15 to 20 messages on my phone. I know everyone tried in his own way to make me feel better, and for some all the distraction helps them over a rough time, but nothing anyone could do or say changed the way I felt. I just didn't know how I would face life without Tom. People would remind me of all the good memories I must have. Memories are great when you can share them with the person you made them with, but when he's gone, thinking of them makes you sadder—makes you long to have him there again.

We held a memorial mass at St. Anthony's church in Fairfield. Again I was stunned by the number of people who packed the church and the distances some of them had traveled. They came from 3M, from the Armory, from the tennis club where I worked. (In fact, the owner closed the club for the day, knowing none of his staff would show up.) Standing at the entrance to the church I was amazed to see Todd Martin, Patrick McEnroe, Carlos Fleming (James's agent who cut short his vacation in Greece), and Mike Nakajima from Nike who endured six hours on a plane from Oregon and had to fly right back as soon as the service ended.

Coping with Grief

I selected the hymns for the service. I especially wanted the prayer of St. Francis, which pleads

O Master, grant that I may never seek
So much to be consoled as to console,
·To be understood as to understand,
To be loved as to love with all my soul.

These words describe exactly the way Tom had lived his life, always putting others' needs before his own. Not always a regular churchgoer, nevertheless he embodied the essence of Christianity better than many of us who never miss a Sunday. When he did go with me to Mass his favorite part was giving the handshake of peace. After a kiss and a hug to me, he would shake as many hands as possible, an enormous smile lighting up his face.

The Reverend John Baran conducted the service. I had met Father John at my parish church, Our Lady of Assumption. After he was transferred to St. Anthony's I often made the trip to his church to hear him speak. When I first heard his sermons they had impressed me, so when I needed advice I sought him out. He had already helped me over some rough times in my life, especially when my mom died.

Father John talked about some of Tom's qualities, notably his perseverance, how until now he refused to let anything get the better of him; his determination, how he always finished what he started and never gave up, and how he pushed me to do the same. He was the only one who persevered at teaching me to drive after many, even the driving school, had failed, and after I had failed the driving test six times. Together we would attempt *The New York Times* Sunday crossword puzzles. If one corner was still blank I would be content to leave it, but he would hound me until I solved it. Now when I do the puzzle I feel I'm letting him down if I don't finish it.

After Father John spoke Thomas and James escorted me to the dais where I talked about Tom's selflessness and about the role model he was for his sons. People all over the world have asked me the secret to raising two such wonderful young men. For that I give all the credit to Tom. I told how proud he was of them, especially of their academic achievements—and how we often wondered how two such ordinary people could have two such extraordinary sons. I concluded with what should have been a comforting quote: "We are such stuff / As dreams are made on, and our little life / Is rounded with a sleep," but even Shakespeare provided little comfort for me.

While I spoke I could hear Thomas crying near my shoulder. Not one to show his emotions I couldn't remember the last time he gave in to tears. He was always the bigger, stronger older brother. When he stepped up to the lectern, he talked of the lessons he learned from his father and his admiration for him. He concluded with, "If I could be half the man he was, I would consider myself a success."

Finally James spoke about his "Superman" who like the comic book hero was supposed to be invincible. We had all admired Tom for his ability to shake off illness and adversity, and we found it difficult to accept something had conquered him. James vowed he would live his life following his father's example and he would teach his children the same values, and in this way his father would be immortal.

For the recessional hymn I had looked up my old school song from England—*Lift up Your Hearts*, and introduced it to the organist. A rousing hymn with an uplifting message, it couldn't dispel our sadness, which carried over to the reception at James's Fairfield house.

Erika had taken care of all the arrangements. All I had to do was sit and chat to anyone who came close. I felt deflated, with no energy to do anything except that. I remember little about the reception but I do recall feeling enormously grateful to Erika for taking over so competently. I found out later the day just happened to be the anniversary of her daughter Sabina's death, always and forever a particularly sad day for her. Erika's concern for me didn't end with that day. Since Tom died I have a standing invitation to Sunday dinner with her family. Knowing grief as she does, she also assured me I could

Coping with Grief

knock on her door any time of the day or night, any time I felt I couldn't cope.

I returned to my part-time job at the tennis club almost immediately. The owner had said I didn't need to but I felt it would help to take my mind off our loss. It certainly wouldn't help to sit home and brood. The first weeks proved an ordeal with so many people, Tom's tennis friends, expressing their sympathy. I know how sincere they all were but it just tended to rub salt in the wound. I couldn't get used to the fact I didn't have to rush off after my shift ended to spend as much time as possible with Tom. Now no one waited for me at home and I often delayed returning to my lonely house.

For several months after Tom died I just went on with my life, doing what had to be done and not much else. After my father's premature death Mom had said she stayed sane by keeping busy; trying to take her mind off it, but her situation was different from mine. She had four children in the house, two of us still in school, as well as her mother to care for—a lot of distractions. Going to work helped me, and I often stayed through most of Erika's four-hour shift so I would have less time alone at home, but I still had too much time to think and grieve.

After Newport Thomas went back on the road as his father had wanted, and I thought James would too, as soon as his arm healed. I remembered James's offer to travel anywhere in the world with him. Attractive as that offer sounded, I knew I had to deal with my own life and try not to lean on him too much. My mom had always been adamant about letting her children go their ways without too much interference and I felt the same way.

I recalled a few years back after one of my rare confessions Father John had given me a book about prayer. For my penance he told me to sit near some water and think about the book. I went to a nearby beach, climbed onto a jetty of rocks and sat down to think. It was mid-winter so I had the beach to myself. As I waited for inspiration I looked down at the seashore. A seagull walked into the water; a wave pushed him back. He tried again, and again a wave forced him back. After a few more attempts he just sat on the next wave and let it carry him along.

My mind went back to that seagull and I realized our lives were a bit like that. We had been buffeted around and now it seemed to me all we could do was let fate take over. Go with the flow. We had no idea things would get a lot worse before they got better.

For the rest of that year I must have been in a daze. I paid little attention to what Thomas and James were doing and barely knew whether they won or lost. It all seemed too trivial to think about.

Because of this attitude I was largely unaware of what was happening to James. My apathy coupled with his trying to shield me from any more hurt combined to keep me ignorant of the situation. I knew he was ill but it wasn't until I read an article about his comeback in the August 28, 2005 issue of *The New York Times* that I realized just how much he had suffered. In the last paragraph of the article James recalls his father told him, "if there's a problem, you're going to fix it, you're not going to complain about it, you're not going to make anyone else a part of your problem." James took Tom's advice to heart. Until much later I had no idea of the severity of James's illness.

It started on a rainy day not long after Tom's death when James and Brian came into the club to practice. I glanced down at the court and noticed James was sitting on the bench. It seemed too soon for him to be taking a break. I left the desk and went down to the court. James was holding his right ear. He told Brian he couldn't go on. This was the first time he had ever cut short a practice, so we were both concerned. He went home to rest, hoping it would soon get better.

The next day I called to check up on James. After a long pause he admitted he was in St. Vincent's Medical Center. (Later he told me he had contemplated not answering the phone when he saw the identity of the caller. He didn't want to add to my grief.) His condition had worsened and his doctor wanted to find out why. He then made light of it, assuring me there was no need to visit him. "You've had enough of hospitals lately, Mom," he said. Of course I dropped everything and went to St. Vincent's.

When I reached the hospital James was hooked up to an IV. A CAT scan had ruled out a tumor but the doctor had no clear diagnosis until a few days later when the rash had begun to recede. The doctor wanted to know if James had experienced stress lately. In what may have been the understatement of the year James admitted he had. While recovering from his own broken neck he had spent six weeks watching his father slowly succumb to cancer. This had been enough to trigger a bout of shingles, which had attacked a facial nerve. The doctor couldn't say whether the nerve was dead, in which case his face would remain paralyzed, or just severely damaged.

The doctor also had no idea how long it would take James to get better. Not realizing how bad it was I expected him to resume playing as soon as possible. He didn't try playing in a tournament again until mid-August, when he went to Washington for the Legg-Mason. When he lost badly in the first round to a player I had never heard of I reasoned he must be a lot sicker than I had thought, but I still didn't know the extent of his illness and I still hoped he would soon be back on the tour again. I felt he needed it to take his mind off his great loss.

On the *Late Show with David Letterman*, after he recovered, he described the pain as 10 times worse than the broken neck. The left side of his face was paralyzed, his left eye stayed open all the time (even when he slept) and he lost hearing in his left ear. Add to that the dizziness he experienced just walking across a room and the metallic taste in his mouth, which made all food taste bad. Besides the physical problems he also had to deal with the uncertainty of the outcome of his illness and of his career and too much time on his hands to ponder his misfortunes and to miss his father, for he was still reeling from that enormous loss. He kept this all to himself for he didn't want to burden me with his troubles.

Mix It Up, Make It Nice

James's many high school and college friends rallied 'round and helped him through a difficult time. Hearing later about how they had been there for him I realized how important those true friends were. Again we were glad he had led a normal childhood and not spent it away from home at a tennis academy, where lasting friendships are rare.

His performance in Washington had made him realize he could not compete in the US Open. It must have been torture for him to have to sit on the sidelines while his friends played in his favorite tournament. All he could do was watch the action on TV. His hordes of local friends felt the disappointment too, for the US Open had become one of the high points in their lives. James loved having his high school friends, his college friends as well as many of my friends and Thomas's friends watching in the stands.

He did take part in Arthur Ashe Kids' Day, an event that takes place on the Saturday before the Open begins. I went to watch it with a friend and it was good to see him chatting and laughing with the other tennis players. I found out later he had been terrified of embarrassing himself because he was still having trouble hitting a ball straight.

Another bitter disappointment in this year of tragedy was missing the Olympics. In an interview in Houston before his accident in Rome, when asked about that event James said, "Singles or doubles, equipment manager, I'll do anything to be a part of it."

During this time whenever I went to his house to visit James put on his brave face, flashed his crooked smile and assured me everything would be okay. Brian told me the doctor's prognosis and managed to sound upbeat about it. Brian, besides being a superlative tennis coach, is also quite the philosopher and an expert at looking on the bright side. Ironically, this talent exhibits itself more in dire situations than in small, unimportant ones. Those he often views with alarm.

James, still hoping to come back, tried another tournament in Delray Beach in September. After losing the

Coping with Grief

first set to the local wildcard he somehow managed to win that match, but in his next round he lost badly, a match he remembers because at one point he swung at the ball and missed it completely. How can you swing and miss with a tennis racket? In all of his Little League baseball games I never once saw him strike out. Had I seen that I would have known something was drastically amiss.

Instead of becoming frustrated he looked up at Thomas and Brian, put his hands on his hips and laughed. This incident and another visit to the doctor convinced him he should abandon tennis for the rest of the year. The doctor had said at least until next year but James, ever the optimist, took it to mean he would start competing again in January 2005. This became his goal.

Brian saw a silver lining to the cloud that seemed to have stationed itself over our family. James's health gradually improved, and he got the green light to start practicing again. Brian decreed he should practice only every other day, and only if he felt up to it. At these practices they would focus on his weak points. James was eager to work again. His work ethic is so strong that not working presents a difficulty for him.

Happy just to be on the court again after so many months of inactivity, James felt ready to work at whatever Brian suggested. Among other things they worked on his backhand making it an offensive weapon, on his defense and on drop shots. Still in the grip of the virus some days went better than others, but Brian helped handle the frustration by reminding him how far he had already come.

Brian also made another wise suggestion. Knowing James became frustrated whenever a practice went badly, and realizing some practices would go badly for James had not yet fully recovered, he told him he should use this time to have some fun. They had several months to practice, a luxury denied to active players on the tour who are compelled to play a certain number of tournaments, so Brian felt James could afford to relax a little.

Mix It Up, Make It Nice

At first James's overactive work ethic balked at the idea, but bowing to Brian's superior wisdom he found relaxing on those off days helped with his frustrations. He spent some time playing golf with his friends, he went to concerts and football games, even took a few short trips. Once again Brian knew what was best for James.

James played two exhibition matches, one in November and another in December, to try to gauge if he would be ready to play at the beginning of 2005 as he anticipated.

Although his friends Robby Ginepri and Mardy Fish had no trouble beating him, James could tell he was getting better and he still resolved to play again in the new year.

Thanksgiving and Christmas were sad affairs. They say the first time you celebrate a holiday without a loved one is the most difficult. After four more holiday seasons without Tom, I find them just as difficult to bear as the first. I told everyone not to expect gifts from me. I had no interest in shopping. In fact that year changed my whole view of Christmas. I no longer had children to shop for and I realized most of the gifts I received I could do without so I did my best to abandon that particular tradition. People call me Scrooge when I tell them I don't do Christmas so I have changed my answer to them. "I celebrate Christmas," I tell them, "but I do it my way." My way is to make it more like Thanksgiving—a day with the family, without the stress of gift-giving—a day to remember what Christmas really means.

That said, I'm not averse to accepting a magnificent gift from James, which has now become almost a tradition. He finances my January trip to New Zealand to visit Ed and Vi, and then on to Australia for the Open where I stay at the Crown Hotel in Melbourne—pure luxury.

Although he won only three matches in three different tournaments "down under" that year, it was a special trip because it marked the beginning of a comeback which none of us in our wildest dreams could have anticipated.

Ah, but a man's reach must exceed his grasp,
Or what's a heaven for?

—ROBERT BROWNING

Chapter 14:
Comeback

JUST AS HE HAD in 2003 when he shaved his head, I believe James began 2005 with a new sense of commitment, and after the year of setbacks and tragedy he had just lived through, a new outlook on life. It was almost like starting over. He had to prove himself again. He had no idea how difficult it might be but with a new, more mature, philosophy, he felt ready to face whatever the future might hold. I read somewhere tragedy leads to self-discovery. James had learned a lot about himself in that dreadful year.

During his injuries and illness his world ranking had plummeted from a high of 22 and would probably drop even further as points from the tournaments he played in the first part of 2004 came off. To maintain your points total you must do as well as or better than you did in the same tournament the preceding year. It's called "defending" your points.

James had won his first three matches at the Australian Open in 2004. Just coming off an illness and a lengthy period with no match play, he would probably not do as well this year. He had also reached the quarterfinals in Indian Wells in March—another feat we could not expect him to duplicate. In fact with his doctor still a little cautious about whether or not he should play and his eyesight still not 100 percent normal, we didn't know what to expect.

James had played the Hopman Cup in Perth three times as a warm-up for the Oz Open. He had become a favorite with the crowd there so he welcomed the chance to play the event again. Like Davis Cup matches this tournament doesn't count in the rankings so there is less pressure—a good way to begin his journey back.

They showed his first match on American television and I remember being almost afraid to watch. He had to play Peter Wessels, a player who was coming to the end of a successful career. James looked unstoppable in the first set, winning it with the loss of only one game. I believe he was feeling the joy of competitive play again. The second set was much closer but James held on to win it in a tiebreaker. We all breathed a sigh of relief. It looked like he was back. James won one more match at that event then flew to New Zealand to compete in the Heineken Open. I had made the trip there again because Ed's heart had been getting weaker and it seemed certain this would be my last chance to see him.

In the previous year with his ranking on the rise, James had often been seeded, thus insuring he would not meet one of the top players in the first rounds of a tournament. Not only was he not seeded in New Zealand but also his ranking had fallen so low he needed a wildcard to get in. Unfortunately, he drew Fernando Gonzalez, the eventual winner, in his first round. He battled hard in the first set only to lose in a tie-breaker, then seemed to run out of steam in the second, losing at 6-1.

James left for Melbourne before I did so he could get used to the unique surface of the Australian Open. When the time came for me to leave, it was an especially poignant goodbye to Ed and Vi at the airport. I hugged my big brother longer than usual, then as I walked to the gate I kept looking back for one last glimpse of him. I think we both knew it would be the last time we would see each other. Tennis was far from my mind as the plane made its way to Australia.

James had drawn Florian Mayer, a young player whose ranking had climbed to 33 in the previous year, for his first-round match. Watching James play that match turned into an incredible experience. After his long absence, after all we had gone through, it was pure joy to see him play like his old self. He won the match with the loss of only three games, 6-1, 6-2, 6-0.

Two days later he had to play his old adversary Lleyton Hewitt. Although Lleyton is Australia's best player, James had plenty of support from the crowd. Each trip I've made to the Australian Open I've been amazed at the increasing numbers of fans who watch James's matches. He has become quite a favorite there.

Incredibly, James won the first set, 6-4, and was on target to win the second when Hewitt came up with some amazing points to take the tiebreaker at 8 points to 6. After that, James, who still seemed to need work on his stamina, lost the next two sets, 6-0 and 6-3.

Later that day a reporter found me in the players' dining area and told me about James's post-match interview. Vastly different from the usual assessment of a match where players typically discuss such earth-shaking topics as whether their backhand had been on that day or whether their first serve was landing in the box, it set the media folks abuzz. All the reporters had been impressed with it and it received a huge write-up in the papers. James talked about the loss of his father, about how his dad is never far from his thoughts. He told them what it meant to him to again play the sport he loves after going through a period of doubt as to whether it would ever happen. He talked about his friends and family and his renewed appreciation of the important things in life. He concluded by putting it all in perspective, "The worst thing that happened to me today; I lost a tennis match."

Returning from "down under" we began to think our elation had been a little premature. James only won one match in his next three tournaments. At times he seemed his old self but there were times when it was all too obvious he hadn't fully recovered his health. His eyesight, so vital to a tennis player, still gave him problems.

At the end of February he entered a tournament in Scottsdale Arizona. Two of my tennis-playing friends who used to live in Connecticut had moved to Mesa. I combined a visit to them with another opportunity to watch James play.

On the first day of play I was walking around the site when I saw James playing with a yellow Labrador puppy. Recalling his days as a dog sitter, I thought, "Only James would find a dog at a tennis tournament." I started playing with the puppy too.

"Whose dog is it, James?"

"It's yours, Mom."

Thinking I needed company in my life, he had bid for the dog at a charity auction the previous evening. At first I wasn't sure this was such a good idea. Did I really want a dog? What happens to the dog when I want to travel?

Nike has become very special to me. Although I do like to travel, I'm home much more than I'm away. We spend a lot of time together and I can't imagine life without her. It was a very good idea.

The tournament authorities had agreed to let Nike come to the site each day James had to play. She had her own ID badge with her picture on it. While James played the officials watched her, and in between matches my friends and I walked her around the grounds. She became a favorite with everyone who saw her. The couple I was

Comeback

staying with, Val and Glenn, also had a dog so they didn't mind having Nike in the house, too.

James lost in the third round and I had to think about getting Nike home. My flight had a "no animals" policy, so I had to put her on a different plane, making sure we would get to Hartford at about the same time. Val and I went to PetSmart and bought a crate for her, as well as a coat to keep her warm and several other doggie items. Getting her settled in the crate took more time than we allowed and I came perilously close to missing my flight. Running as fast as I could through the airport, I began to panic as I wondered what would happen if I missed the plane. There would be no one to claim my dog. I got there in the nick of time. Relieved and breathless, I sank into my seat. My relief proved short-lived, for before we became airborne the stewardess announced there was a glitch and we had to turn back to check it out.

Near tears I told the stewardess, "I have to get there on time to pick up my dog."

Gently, she guided me back to my seat. "Let's find out what's wrong with the plane, then we'll worry about your dog," she said. "I'm sure she'll be all right." Normally, the problem with the plane would have caused me some concern but all I could think about was my dog.

Fortunately it was a minor glitch. Both planes made it to Hartford on time and I was reunited with a very frisky Nike. I had parked my car in a lot away from the airport (I didn't know I would be bringing a dog back with me). I don't know how I managed to get the dog, the crate and my luggage on the bus to the parking lot. By the time I put the dog in the back seat and the crate and the luggage in the trunk, I was so flustered I found myself going the wrong way on the Merritt Parkway. I exited at the first ramp, turned around and made it home without further mishap.

A small dog at first, Nike grew rapidly, topping off at 91 pounds. A typical puppy, she chewed everything she could find. I could deal with the shoes and slippers, but when she destroyed one of my tennis rackets and took chunks

203

out of the furniture, I had to lay down the law. Luckily she soon put her puppy ways behind her and now limits her chewing to anything and everything edible.

About this time some friction had set in at the tennis club where Erika and I worked. Because of this, on two separate occasions I threatened to quit. Each time I walked out Erika had become upset so I went back. She had already had so much pain in her life I could never knowingly cause her more. I gritted my teeth and kept working. In March the situation worsened and Erika resigned. Now there was no reason for me to stay so I left too.

We had both enjoyed working at the club but after some initial sadness we agreed it was a good move. Erika's oldest daughter Tanya, pregnant with twins, had moved temporarily to Atlanta so now Erika would be able to visit her. I still felt I had little to live for but I was happy to spend more time with my dog, whose happiness was gradually becoming my main purpose in life.

I made several attempts to train Nike but I soon realized I needed Tom's firm hand. He had been the one who disciplined our sons, and he would have been as firm with a dog. Thomas and James call me "the softie." I usually gave in to them and I treated Nike the same. Every trainer I tried remarked on Nike's intelligence and on how trainable she was but I could never bring myself to be mean to her.

Perhaps if I had, the accident wouldn't have happened. Playing in the yard one day in April, Nike, running at top speed with me encouraging her to go even faster, cannoned into me. Her head collided with my right knee and her head proved the harder. It hurt and felt like something had become dislocated. I thought walking would snap it back. I soon realized I couldn't put any weight on that leg. I hopped into the house and called Erika. She came over at once, took me to the hospital and stayed there all day with me, only leaving to get me a cup of tea and a sandwich. After lengthy waits, x-rays, then more long waits, they told me I had a broken tibia. Because I had eaten the sandwich they couldn't operate at once, which proved providential. They sent me home with a cast on and told me to call the next day. When James heard of the accident, he insisted I go to The Hospital for Special Surgery in New York City where he had gone for treatment of his broken neck.

The doctors there gave me two options—let the break heal by itself and risk less mobility and the threat of arthritis, or submit to surgery and have the bones aligned properly. With the surgery it would be a longer rehab time but they guaranteed better results. I had been planning a trip to Dallas to see my son Chris and then on to Houston to watch James play in a tournament. If I chose the surgery, I would have to cancel the trip. It was a tough decision, but heeding Brian's wise counsel I chose the longer route.

Not only did Brian give me good advice, he also helped enormously when none of the family was available. On the day of the surgery with Thomas and James in Houston for a tournament, Brian drove me to the hospital and waited with me until they took me away. After the lengthy operation, I was surprised to see Brian there when they wheeled me into the recovery room.

"Have you been here all this time?" I asked him.

He had driven home but then felt someone should be there when I woke up so he drove back to the hospital, a journey of more than an hour. As I've said before, Brian is more than just a coach.

Before I went into the operating room, the doctor told me he had just had a long talk with my son.

"Oh, you talked to Thomas?" I asked, for I had put his name down as next of kin.

"No, James called me."

That moved me to tears. "He's lost one parent. He doesn't want to lose another." The doctor put an arm around me and assured me that wouldn't happen.

The next six weeks proved difficult, especially with an active puppy to care for, but family and friends rallied around and helped. Since I couldn't visit him, Chris came from Dallas and spent one whole week with me after I left the hospital. During that week he did everything—cleaned the house, shopped for groceries, made meals, did the laundry and walked Nike. Most of all, he raised my spirits, helping me over the most difficult time. After he left, my oldest son Howard came over with his two daughters to help. Thomas came whenever he could, but seeing all the friends who continually stopped by to help and to bring me food, he could see I didn't need him too often.

JAMES'S RANKING now hovered around 200 and for the next three tournaments he needed a wildcard to get in. He was playing well but just like his early days on the tour he was losing in close matches, which did nothing for his ranking. When the tournament schedule moved overseas for the clay court season he could no longer expect wildcards (they typically go to the local talent), so he and Brian decided he should go back to the Challengers to try to earn some points.

James first played in Tunica Mississippi and came perilously close to losing a match in the second round. He eked out a win with a 6-4 victory in the third set and then continued on to win the tournament, giving him 50 points. His second Challenger was at Forest Hills in New York, just a short drive from Fairfield. Brian and Thomas drove me down each day. I still had a cast on so we took the wheelchair.

Although it was a little inconvenient maneuvering my way around, this provided a welcome change to spending my days either on the sofa or in the back yard. James won his match each day so we spent most of that week there. The 100 points he gained in these two weeks would boost his ranking, but the points wouldn't register in time for the next tournament—the French Open. Without the benefit of a wildcard James had to play in the qualifying tournament, which began in just two days.

While Thomas drove me and my wheelchair home, James and his coach rushed to JFK to board a plane to Paris, hoping to arrive in time for James to have at least

Comeback

one day to get over his jet lag and practice on the Roland Garros courts. Fortunately the final match at Forest Hills went only two short sets and James had brought his luggage with him. They reached the airport in time to get the overnight plane to France.

James won three rounds in the qualifying draw, which put him into the main draw. He won his first round and began his second round well by winning the first two sets, but then his old nemesis leg cramps began to bother him and although he fought hard, especially in the fifth set, he went down, 6-4.

Because James typically doesn't play his best on clay yet had played reasonably well in these last three tournaments, we thought he had put his illness behind him and was on his way to regaining his old form. His ranking, which fell to a low of 210 in April, had begun a slow climb back but he needed to go deep in the next tournaments to get close to his former ranking. We hoped with the grass court season coming up and his favorite hard court surface right behind it this would soon happen.

Our hopes were dashed when James went through the months of June and July winning only three matches in five tournaments, with one of the wins coming when his opponent retired. With his ranking too low for a seeded position he could have drawn highly ranked players in the first rounds, but he was getting good draws yet still losing to players we felt he should have been able to beat. We began to wonder if he had truly recovered from his bad year or if, after such a long hiatus, he could make a comeback. Had we known what the next six weeks would bring our gloom would have lightened considerably.

At the beginning of August he played the Legg-Mason tournament in Washington DC, the scene of his first and only ATP title. I don't know if the memory of that victory inspired him but he won his way to the finals with impressive wins over highly ranked players before losing to Andy Roddick, 7-5, 6-3. Accepting the runner-up trophy, after thanking all the appropriate people, he told the huge crowd his mom would celebrate her birthday on the following day and asked them all to serenade me with a chorus of "Happy Birthday." As if that weren't embarrassing enough, he then told everyone my age. Later I asked him why he had to share that particular piece of information.

"I thought you were proud of it," he said.

That may be, but I didn't necessarily need to share it with a stadium full of perfect strangers.

The points James gained in Washington brought his ranking up to 67, but points are slow to register and he still needed a wildcard for his next three tournaments. In Cincinnati he drew Roger Federer in the first round. He lost the match by a score of 7-6, 7-5, a respectable score against the best player on the tour. After the match James had the grace to admit he thought Roger might have played at 75 percent of his ability.

After that quick exit James came back to Fairfield with time to prepare for his next tournament, the Pilot Pen in New Haven Connecticut, just a 20-minute ride from Fairfield. Formerly known as the Hamlet, James had played in this tournament in 2003 when it took place in August on Long Island just before the US Open. I recalled that tournament as the first one Tom felt strong enough to attend after his operation. Each day we watched James win another round, only losing in the final match to Paradorn Srichaphan. What I remember most about that tournament was how different Tom's photo on the ID badge looked. Always spare, he had now lost a lot of weight and muscle tone and looked much older than his years.

James was delighted to be playing in New Haven where his friends and family could come out and support him. Even though he needed a wildcard to enter the tournament, Anne Worcester, the Tournament Director, realized James, coming from Connecticut, would generate plenty of publicity. She generously donated a section of the center court to James's fans and came up with a title for it—the "J-Block." It proved an enormous success and has now become an institution at the US Open where James usually provides them with one of the suites.

Comeback

James continued his good form and was able to repay Anne's generosity by winning the tournament. This gave him 200 points and boosted his ranking to 49. From a low of 210 in April, in just four months he had moved up 161 places. I still remember the look on his face when he won that last point. His smile seemed to come up from his socks as he flashed it all around the stadium to the hordes of friends, old and new. Then he came over to the family box to give me a long hug. I told him how proud his dad would be and he had the same thought on his mind.

With the US Open beginning just two days later we weren't sure what to expect from James. After playing a match every day in New Haven we thought he might be too tired to continue his good form. His recent points still hadn't registered so he went in as a wildcard and had to rely on the luck of the draw.

The momentum continued. James's first match was against a big-serving lefty, Greg Rusedski, who had made short work of him in their first encounter in March 2000 when James won only two games. James surprised us by winning in three sets, and then two days later posted another straight set win over Igor Andreev. His next opponent, Rafael Nadal, at that time the second-best player in the world, came fresh from his triumphs at the French Open and a Masters event in Montreal where he had beaten Agassi in the final. I didn't check the odds but it must have been something like a thousand to one against James.

With the J-Block going crazy up in their suite, James won the first set. They cooled a little after Nadal took the second. When James won the third, then got a service break in the fourth, I wouldn't have been at all surprised to see someone fall out of that box right onto Arthur Ashe stadium. They were positively manic. Sitting opposite in the family box I was torn between watching them and watching the match. When James won the last point pandemonium broke loose. "I could have yelled at the top of my voice, and no one would have heard," said James. He also said he wished every one of them could have the feeling he had at that moment. As he sank to his knees he must have been thinking just one year earlier they had all been in his living room, helping to raise his spirits and not knowing if they would ever watch him play again.

Up in the family box we all congratulated each other and I couldn't stop the tears. If only Tom could have been there to see this. How I ached to share another victory hug with him. I knew James's thoughts were similar to mine. Reporters bombarded me before I could leave my seat. "How do you feel?" What could I say? To see James's smile spread over his entire face, not just the right side; to see joy after some of the darkest days of his young life. Nothing pleases a mother more than seeing her children happy. In the box next to me, Thomas was just as ecstatic. It was a euphoric moment.

In the next round James came from behind to beat Tommy Robredo and found himself in the quarterfinals of the US Open for the first time. In an interview he said if someone had told him last year that one year later he would lose in the quarterfinals of the Open without winning a single game he would have taken it in a heartbeat.

Reporters had a field day with this event. An all-American affair, it pitted the ever-popular Andre Agassi, nearing the end of his legendary career, against the improbable wildcard born in Yonkers and claimed by New Yorkers as a favorite son—a dream match for the media.

If possible, the match, when it finally started around 10 p.m., exceeded all the hype. Improbably, James took the first two sets. I don't know how others in the box felt, but I'm sure Brian and I had similar thoughts: Andre won't go away this easily. Of course we were right. After those first two sets, a change came over the crowd. Now perceiving Andre as the underdog, they threw their support to him. He responded by winning the next two sets. The fifth set became one of those events destined to replay during rainouts long after James hangs up his rackets.

It stayed neck-and-neck until James broke Andre's serve to go up 5-4. Now he could serve out the set. Again

Comeback

Andre wouldn't go away. Known as one of the best in the game at returning serve, he hung on and broke James back: 5-all. Agassi held and so did James to make the score 6-all, and this epic match would now be decided by a tiebreaker. In the wee hours of the morning that vast Arthur Ashe Stadium remained packed. Quickly, James took a 3-0 lead. We watched from the box, barely breathing. James looked up into the blackness beyond the lights and mouthed something. Watching the tape later you could easily read his lips: "I love you, Dad." If this were fiction James would have to come out the winner but there was no storybook ending here. Andre fought back and went ahead, 6-5. James fought off one match point to make it 6-all. Then Andre hit two winners in a row to win the match.

What thoughts went through James's head as he sat on the sidelines while Agassi acknowledged the crowd's adulation? I watched him kiss the chain on his left wrist, his thoughts still with his father. Then the announcer presented James to the crowd amid deafening applause. As Andre and James embraced at the net Andre told the crowd the real winner tonight was tennis. When was the last time Center Court stayed packed at 2 a.m.?

James had little time to brood about his loss. Patrick McEnroe felt James was ready to play Davis Cup again—a semifinal match against Belgium, on clay in Belgium. This event has always been special to James and knowing how much it meant to him to play again for his country after a hiatus of more than two years I felt I had to make the trip. I didn't consider the expense or the inconvenience of such a long trip for such a short time. I knew I had to go.

On the first day of competition, just seeing a smiling James bound into the arena, the Stars and Stripes waving on each side, made the trip worthwhile. I couldn't stop the tears as I thought about how much this meant to him and what he had gone through to get back to this point. I cried for his happiness and I cried for my sadness at not having his father there with me to share this incredible moment.

James played Olivier Rochus on the slow clay surface that admirably suits his game. The points seemed interminable but Rochus prevailed. Then Andy Roddick stepped in and saved the day and at the end of the weekend the US came away with a 4-1 victory.

Two weeks later, back on his favorite surface—indoor, hard—James claimed a third title, this one in Stockholm Sweden. During his run to the trophy he notched a straight-set win over Olivier Rochus. After the final match I had a congratulatory call from Swedish tennis star Mats Wilander. He told me this had been one of his favorite tournaments and I should plan to attend on the following year if James played in it again. I took his advice.

James played two more tournaments but seemed ready for a break. Now in the top 20, he had already reached higher than before his illness. We looked forward to 2006. James didn't disappoint us.

The best is yet to be,

—ROBERT BROWNING

Chapter 15:
A Dream Come True

THE YEAR 2006 began on a sad note. After quietly celebrating the holidays again, I prepared once more to visit Ed and Vi. I had not intended to make the long trip this year but against all his doctors' predictions Ed had survived another year. I felt I had to see him one more time.

The phone call came after I had bought my ticket, just a few days before my departure date. Ed's heart had finally given out. When my mom died early in January 1997, I remember thinking how even in death she seemed thoughtful of others—she waited until after the holidays and now Ed had done the same. I cried with Vi, said some inadequate words of comfort, then asked if the funeral could wait until I arrived. I called Nin and Albert and offered to represent them at the service. Both sent remembrances of their brother for me to read and I wrote my own piece.

The funeral service was an upbeat affair. Ed had lived almost 81 years and had enjoyed a happier life than most. Never one to let anything bother him, he had faced his approaching death with the same tranquility. In one of his hospital stays he had penned a poem to be read at his funeral. The gist of it was we shouldn't grieve for him because now he was better off than the rest of us. When my turn came I read what Nin had written about how Ed protected her when they were growing up. Albert recalled how special it felt when they went fishing together. An English Literature professor, he couldn't resist a quote from Shakespeare: "He was a man, take him for all in all, / I shall not look upon his like again." Albert had adored his big brother.

I spoke of how Ed teased me mercilessly when I was young but how I didn't mind because it was never malicious. "Of course you win all your races, Bet. Just stick out that long, scrawny neck and you're already ahead of everyone." I spoke of how with my visits we had become much closer over the last few years. I had been impressed with how many of his friends and family in their cards of condolence emphasized his gentle nature— not just a gentleman but also a gentle man, and that triggered a quote in my head.

> *His life was gentle; and the elements*
> *So mix'd in him, that Nature might stand up,*
> *And say to all the world,* This was a man!

Shakespeare summed up Ed's life much better than I could. Vi liked that quotation so much it is etched on his tombstone.

While I stayed a little longer in New Zealand, James continued his comeback by winning a tournament in Sydney. That brought his total of titles to four. Before the end of 2006 that total had increased to eight. He added the fifth in March at the Tennis Channel Open in Las Vegas, with his first pro tour win over Lleyton Hewitt in the final match. At the Indianapolis tournament in July he and Andy Roddick played a thrilling final with James prevailing in the third-set tiebreaker by a score of 7-5. James won again in Bangkok in September, then with Marilyn, Brian's mother, and me in the audience, he defended his Stockholm title in October for a total of eight altogether.

With the two wins early in the year his ranking rose into the teens. At the Indian Wells tournament in March after winning his first three rounds he needed one more win to become a top-10 player. He won not one but the next two matches before losing in the final to Roger Federer. The media began speculating about how much further he could go. We soon found out. By the summer his ranking rose to five and for the rest of 2006 he became the number-one American player.

I thought back to his junior days about how excited we were when we first saw his name at the top of the national list. Then I recalled how he surprised us all when he blossomed to become the top college player in just his second year. All that changed when he turned pro and suffered many more losses than wins for such a long time. At that point we would never have predicted he could rise to these lofty heights. His perseverance and hard work had now paid huge dividends. Throughout these past two comeback years I firmly believe James's inspiration has been the memory of his father and the lessons he taught him.

After Indian Wells James's next tournament was in Miami. There he reached the quarterfinals where he again lost to Federer. Although Roger won in straight sets, the first went to a tiebreaker and the second ended with a score of 6-4, only one break of serve. James was getting closer. I watched the match prior to this one on TV. After James lost the first set the camera turned on the area where his entourage sat. Thomas was directing several people to change their seats. Mary Carillo, the announcer, expressed her disbelief. "He's a Harvard graduate and he thinks changing their seats will make a difference?" When I reported this to Thomas, his terse comment was, "Did it work?" Apparently he didn't try it for the next match. He probably realized Federer would overcome even this particular form of voodoo.

By the end of August when the US Open came around again, as the current top American the media asked James to speculate on his prospects and if he felt he could rise even higher in the rankings. His response was he never sets specific goals. His one goal is to get better. "If I would have said I want to be top 10 in the world when I was 210, people would have laughed at me," he said. "That's why I always say I don't set goals like that."

© and photo by Ray Giubilo

US Open 2006. James wins his fourth-round match.

After winning his first three matches he found himself in the quarterfinals again. Last year's match with Agassi was tough; this one could be much tougher—Federer again. James played his best tennis and even had Roger looking a little apprehensive at one point. For the first time James won a set, but Federer prevailed and won the match.

By the end of the year James was in the running to go to the final tournament of the season—the Masters Cup, to be held in Shanghai. Only the top eight players are invited. James eked his way in as the eighth player after Tommy Haas had to retire from his last tournament with a stomach virus. Knowing this might be our only chance, Thomas and I hurriedly made plans to go with him. We needed a special visa to travel to China but with help from James's agent we procured it in time.

A Dream Come True

That turned into a trip to remember. I had never before visited any country in Asia and didn't know what to expect. After an interminable wait in the airport we emerged into the daylight at about 3:30, but where was the daylight? Granted it was November when the days are becoming shorter but it seemed much later than mid-afternoon. A haze seemed to envelop the entire city. A taxi took us to our hotel. I concluded it must be rush hour for there was more traffic than I have ever seen anywhere. Most of the cars are smaller than ours and they constantly go in and out of traffic, continually honking their horns. This kept up throughout the entire ride, which was well over an hour. I discovered later this goes on all the time, not just rush hour. I decided if I lived in this country I would never have the courage to drive.

The eight players are divided into two groups. James's group comprised Rafael Nadal, Nikolay Davydenko and Tommy Robredo, while Federer, Roddick, David Nalbandian and Ivan Ljubičić made up the other group. You have to play each player in your group, then one of the winners from the other group if you get to the semifinals.

Going into the tournament James told a reporter "I'm not one of the last guys to qualify; I am the last guy. I'm the guy that's supposed to be the easy match-up. I'm just happy to be here." Then he added, "Now I have been given the opportunity I am going to try to take it."

His first match showed he was by no means the "easy match-up." Playing against Nadal, James took the first set at 6-4, then lost his serve twice and found himself looking at a 4-0 deficit in the second set. He bore down, broke back twice and took the set to a tiebreaker, which he won without losing a point. In his next match Davydenko initially looked unstoppable. He won the first set and had one service break in the second with a chance to break again, which would have virtually put the match out of reach. James held his serve then broke back and eventually won the match, making him the first player in the semis. The next day, in a meaningless match Robredo beat him.

Mix It Up, Make It Nice

James saved his best effort for the semis against David Nalbandian, the defending champion. This match reminded me of when he played in Washington against Agassi in 2002 when it appeared he could do no wrong. James played with the same kind of magic and for most of the match the outcome was never in doubt. The last player to qualify for the tournament, James had made it to the finals.

Each morning of our stay James, Brian, Thomas, Mark Merklein (the trainer) and I enjoyed breakfast in a room high above the city the hotel had set aside for tournament personnel. On the first morning they were trying to come up with a suitable penalty in the event James got to the finals. They had abandoned several suggestions before James came up with the plan they should all grow a moustache as soon as the holidays ended and wear it for as long as James stayed in the Australian Open. Smiling a little at the improbability of having to do this, they all agreed. When the improbable happened, even with the thought of having to make good on their bet they felt it was worth it.

In the final match there was no stopping Federer. He won the match by a score of 6-0, 6-3, 6-4. Even Roger had to admit he played a fantastic match. "I had to laugh at times today at how well I was playing," he said. James had nothing but praise for the champion. He said he played his best, but Roger was "just better in every sense and every facet of the game."

Because of the Masters tournament, James had less off time this year but he still managed to fit in several charity events before coming home to Connecticut for the holidays and a well-earned rest. This had been a year to remember. Besides his meteoric rise in the rankings, James also published a book. *Breaking Back* chronicled his comeback from the events of 2004 and landed on the best-seller list. In addition because of that incredible comeback he received an ESPY nomination for "Comeback Player of the Year."

The ESPY awards go to athletes in all the major sports for outstanding performances in their fields. The award

A Dream Come True

ceremony takes place in California in midsummer and has become a glittering occasion. James didn't win the award but that didn't stop him from enjoying the opportunity to mingle with all the greats of the athletic world.

With the results from Shanghai, James's ranking rose to an unbelievable four in the world. How proud Tom would be of his youngest son. On New Years Eve 2006 our reflections were mostly positive.

After a year like that it seemed anything else would be anti-climactic. James had already exceeded his own wildest dreams and done more than we would ever have thought possible but there was more excitement to come. He won two more titles in 2007, bringing his total to 10. He defended his Sydney title in January and then delighted the J-Block by taking the Pilot Pen again.

© and photo by Ray Giubilo

James at the 2007 Sony Ericsson Open

The most exciting, most rewarding event came close to the end of the year. Patrick McEnroe had kept the same Davis Cup team— Andy Roddick, James and the Bryan brothers—for a number of matches. They had come close, but had not been able to bring the Cup back to the US. In November 2007 they reached the final against Russia. The last time they played Russia was on clay in Russia, so this time it would be at home, and the home team could pick the surface. McEnroe chose indoor carpet, a surface especially suited to Andy and James's games.

A huge contingent of fans traveled from Connecticut to Portland Oregon to give support. Brian's mother Marilyn and I traveled together and it seemed like the entire J-

Block was on the same plane. The flight from LaGuardia was delayed and we missed our connection in Chicago by 20 minutes. We all scooted through the airport frantically looking for the next plane to Portland. Already resigned to missing Andy's match we began to worry we would miss James's too. On that later flight we couldn't wait for the plane to land so we could get an update on the match from a cell phone. Marilyn and I, not versed in the latest technology, kept asking some of the younger fans what was happening. Andy was going through Dmitry Tursunov much too quickly. We were almost willing him to lose a set, just to delay the start of James's match. No luck. Andy won in straight sets. I'm not sure how the others got to the site, but Marilyn and I had a car waiting for us (courtesy of the USTA). We crammed as many others as we could in with us and took off. By the time we reached the stadium, James was ahead 3-0 in the first set against Mikhail Youzhny.

We settled into our seats, directly behind the bench where the US team sat. My son Chris and his friend Ken had come from Dallas and Marilyn and I had seats next to them. They had no flight problems so they filled us in on the first match. James's match was close and every time there was a tense moment I would grip Chris's arm. I knew how much this meant to James. With James up two sets to one and comfortably ahead in the fourth set tiebreaker, Chris said, "Feel better now?" "Not yet," I told him and sure enough James proceeded to lose three points in a row to make the score close again. When he ended our misery and won the last point everyone knew this match had virtually sealed the championship.

After the US bench emptied and his teammates climbed all over him, James turned toward the crowd and I could read his lips: "Where's my mom?" I went down courtside and we shared a long, tearful victory hug. I thought back to his elation after that first Davis Cup win and all their efforts since and I knew what a special moment this was. James admitted later it was one of the greatest moments of his career.

A Dream Come True

As expected the Bryan brothers easily won their doubles match the next day and finally after a 12-year drought this team had brought the Davis Cup back to the United States—a thrilling way to end the year.

Chris, Thomas, me.
Davis Cup celebration, Oregon 2007.

In 2008 James achieved another dream when he competed in the Beijing Olympics. The games began on August 8. For weeks before you couldn't turn on the TV without seeing "8-08-08" flashing on the screen. On my birthday (August 8) and on Mother's Day I know I will get four phone calls (my sons know how I feel about greeting cards; they are forbidden). I often speculate as to who will be first—usually Chris. In 2008 James got there first. The phone rang at 6:30 a.m., just as I was getting ready to walk Nike.

"Happy birthday, Mom."

"James, how did you know I'd be up?"

"You're always up Mom. We're waiting to process."

On that warm summer morning, that gave me a chill. I knew how much it meant to him to march under the

221

American flag. After being denied in 2004 he would now have the thrill of marching in the Olympic procession. Another dream come true.

While some of the tennis players opted to stay in plush hotels James preferred Olympic Village where he could mingle with athletes from other sports. Playing inspired tennis in the muggy Beijing atmosphere he won his way to the semifinals. After an improbable win over Federer in the quarterfinals he had his sights set on a medal.

The next match against Fernando Gonzalez developed into an epic battle in which James won the first set, 6-4, lost the second, 7-5, then played a marathon third set which ended with Gonzalez prevailing by a score of 11-9. This set was marred by a disputed point when the score stood at 9-all. James hit a shot that went out, but not before it tipped his opponent's racket, which would give James the point. The umpire failed to see this (the camera did) but Gonzalez wouldn't admit it and he went on to win the set against his disillusioned opponent.

I've seen similar incidents, particularly in the women's game, and I wonder about the ethics of those involved. Is it really worth sacrificing your integrity for a game? Apparently some think so. (Is that why "nice guys finish last?") James spoke to the media about his disappointment. "That's a disappointing way to exit the tournament, when you not only lose the match, but you lose a little faith in your fellow competitor. Playing in the Olympics, in what's considered a gentleman's sport, that's a time to call it on yourself." He added had he behaved that way with his dad watching he would have had to sit down for a week. When I heard of the incident I had the same thought. Tom could tolerate the temper tantrums in James's youth when he only hurt himself, but he never condoned unsportsmanlike behavior towards an opponent.

It took James a long time to get over that huge disappointment and it reflected in his play for the rest of the year. He seemed mentally, physically and emotionally drained.

A Dream Come True

After almost three years as one of the top 10 players in the tennis world, James's ranking has now slipped considerably. Some critics seem to think he has seen his best years and his active career is coming to an end. I believe, with determination and hard work he still has several years of great tennis ahead of him.

That said, I won't be upset whenever James decides to retire and lead a more normal life. I would love to see both Thomas and James happily married. Both have had several girlfriends, but the bar is in a lofty position. James once told me the reason it's taking him a long time to find the right mate is because he wants something as good as his mom and dad had. If they could both achieve that it would make me happier than having them add a Grand Slam trophy to their other awards.

I often reflect on all the fringe benefits that have come their way because we introduced them to the game we love. Besides the obvious financial rewards and the opportunities for travel all over the globe there are others that mean a lot to them. When James papered his bedroom walls with Michael Jordan posters would he ever in his wildest dreams have believed someday MJ would sit in his house with him playing poker or they would be on the golf course together? As a teenager trying to sneak into the US Open could he have envisioned someday he would count Sampras, Courier and Agassi among his friends? Loving many other sports, especially team sports, James has enjoyed the privilege of taking batting practice with the Mets and the Yankees and the opportunity to befriend such players as Derek Jeter and David Wright.

The acclaim they receive makes it possible for them to raise money for their favorite charities, most especially the fund for cancer research in their father's name. James also enjoys being able to repay in a big way those friends who stayed with him through his misfortunes; and both my boys take such good care of me I often wonder what I did to deserve it.

In the summer of 2009 they suggested I needed to move to a smaller house. "Why would I move at my time of life?" I asked, but the more I thought about it the more the idea appealed to me so I agreed it was a good idea but I would first have to sell my house. "No Mom," James said. "I want to buy you a house."

That October I moved into that smaller house. It's half a mile from the beach and a 20-minute walk to James's Fairfield house. It has a large fenced-in backyard (for Nike), bordered by 22 rose bushes. It sits close to the center of town and just around the corner from Erika's house. As an added bonus it also happens to lie in Father John's parish, St. Anthony's.

On the day I moved Chris called and anxiously asked how I felt, leaving our house after 22 years. "I had no regrets," I told him. The good memories from the happy years we spent there are so tinged with sadness I was glad to get away from them. I couldn't come down the stairs without remembering Tom tripping down them every morning or become reconciled to never hearing his car come around the driveway again. I cry a lot less in my new home and if I do feel low Nike and I take a walk to the beach where the water always lifts my spirits.

I recently read an article about the actor Michael Caine. It talked about one of his movies that didn't do too well. His response to his critics was although the movie wasn't good, the house he bought for his mother with the proceeds was very good. That's how I feel about James's critics. All the good he has done for so many people because of his career in tennis far outweighs the fact his latest results haven't been up to expectations.

On a smaller scale tennis has been good to Thomas too. During his years on tour he became known as likeable, dependable and intelligent and made a ton of contacts that have proved beneficial in his present career. Because of this he is able to avoid getting into the rut of a 9-5 job, which to Thomas would be anathema.

Despite the recognition our boys enjoy (sometimes more people recognize Thomas than James, probably because of his hair), they have never abandoned the values their father espoused and passed on to them. They appreciate the good fortune that has come their way because of their involvement in tennis but they keep it in perspective. To quote James: "How well you hit a tennis ball is just a little thing. The rest of it, that's your life, that's who you are."

In 2010, the ATP awarded James the Arthur Ashe Humanitarian Award. James didn't mention it; I found out when I read it in the paper. I mentioned to Brian of all the awards handed out I'm happiest to see him get that one. "What about 'Player of the Year?'" he asked. At first I agreed, then said, "No, that's just tennis—this means a lot more."

I'm proud of the way our children developed. When people admire their characters, I tell them it's all due to the way Tom brought them up. He knew the right way to rear children. The last sentence he wrote to his boys before he left us: "So many nights I lay in bed worried while you were out. You thought I was nuts with my house rules. It was because of my love and fear for you."

That sums it up. Discipline tempered with love. The right formula. Thanks, Tom.

Mix It Up, Make It Nice

Epilogue

DAVID FOSTER WALLACE SAID "... only wackos would make the financial and temporal sacrifices necessary to let their offspring become good enough at something to turn pro at it ...," but I like to think Tom and I avoided the "wacko" designation by leaving it up to our offspring to decide if and when they deemed the sacrifices necessary.

Realizing Thomas and James might some day be National material, Brian asked them, "Is there anything I can say to convince you to practice more than twice a week?" Speaking for both of them Thomas, who had a slew of other interests, replied definitively, "No."

Mix It Up, Make It Nice

They proceeded at their own pace, with no pressure to produce results. When they began to excel on the college scene and enjoyed the benefits of Geoff Grant's experiences on the tour, they saw tennis as a career possibility. Then they accepted the sacrifices; then the hard work began. Their choice, not ours.

I'm 100 percent sure this attitude has been the key to their ultimate success.

One Set, One Match, One Cure

I WOULD LIKE TO mention the Thomas Blake Sr. Memorial Research Fund, which James established in memory of his father.

By the time Tom's cancer was discovered it was too late for a cure. In cooperation with the Memorial Sloan-Kettering Cancer Center, the Blake Research Fund provides resources for the early diagnosis and treatment of cancer in the hope that other cancer victims may have better outcomes.

If you would like to help you can make a contribution on line or by mail. It can be made to honor or memorialize someone dear to you.

For more information:

by phone: 646-227-3526

by e-mail: blakeresearchfund@mskcc.org

or visit the Memorial Sloan-Kettering Cancer Center web site at www.mskcc.org and click on "How to Help."

Mix It Up, Make It Nice